SYMPHONY #1

SYMPHONY #1 IN A MINOR KEY: A MEDITATION ON TIME AND PLACE

ALAN A. BLOCK

iUniverse, Inc.
Bloomington

Symphony #1 in a Minor Key
A Meditation on Time and Place

iUniverse books may be ordered through booksellers or by contacting:

iUniverse
1663 Liberty Drive
Bloomington, IN 47403
www.iuniverse.com
1-800-Authors (1-800-288-4677)

ISBN: 978-1-4759-0779-7 (sc)
ISBN: 978-1-4759-0781-0 (hc)
ISBN: 978-1-4759-0780-3 (ebk)

Library of Congress Control Number: 2012906093

Printed in the United States of America

iUniverse rev. date: 04/02/2012

*To Barb Kuttler who supported and inspired me
throughout the writing of this book;
to Ludwig van Beethoven, whose work enthralls me;
to Emma and Anna Rose whose lives have inspired mine.*

CONTENTS

PROGRAM NOTES

Before I began this present work, I had already spent forty years exploring the world linguistically. In my daily life, I studied and expressed the world predominantly through the spoken and written word. Trained as a literary exegete in the English Departments of Roanoke College, Hofstra and St. John's University, I learned the language of literature and criticism, and I have used it since to explore and explain my world. Under the tutelage of a few wonderful teachers and scholars, I read and have continued to read voluminously and eclectically in a variety of genres.

For one, I learned how to read and to write as if these things mattered, and as if the engagement with literature would change the world. To study any literary work was to engage in an aesthetic experience that would lead to a truth that could not be realized in the language and thought of science. Trained as a New Critic, I came to expect the poem—any piece of literature, really—to present a unified, organic structure that the learned and trained critic could meticulously analyze to reveal how all components of the work interrelated, and how together all of the elements coalesced to create a single and singular theme, or idea. This *idea* was to be based wholly in the text and would exist independent of reader, history, biography or other material or influence outside of that text.

Searching for eternal Truth and Beauty, I vigorously and expectantly studied texts. Everything for which I searched existed, I believed, somewhere in a book. That book, I trusted—perhaps it was yet lost—when expertly read would offer inestimable insight into the realization of my dreams. I immersed myself in the study of literary texts as if my life depended on it. Somewhere out there was the book—if only it could be found—that would provide me answers to some of the more difficult questions my living had raised. Trusting in print, I consecrated my life to the efficacy of the written word, and I searched for exactly that book which would comment unquestionably on my existence. From this stance, I lived, and from this stance, I taught. And I remained convinced that if that book was not found today, it would certainly be recovered tomorrow. Godot carried it towards me.

And for a while I was happy. I knew Truth and Beauty.

Soon, however, I learned that New Criticism and its methods were themselves historically and hence, ideologically situated as an interpretive system, and its claims to truth and beauty were problematic at best. In the next years, I learned to practice other forms of literary criticism. At various times, I might be concerned with how the text shaped my response to it, or how the book offered a window into the historical moment in which it was created, or how it perhaps provided insight into the psychological state of the author and even the reader. I might be led to wonder how my present cultural position enabled a specific reading of text. Even deconstructive criticism attempted to show how meaning could never be fixed in the text itself but had to derive from the entire event of textuality. Regardless of the method I employed, however, I dealt inevitably with the theme of any particular piece of literature. Theme—I called it sometimes meaning or idea—was always a presence. Regardless of the interpretive strategy, discerning the theme of the *entire* work informed the practice of my reading and pedagogy. Such study was also my pleasure, though I no longer expected to find Truth and Beauty in texts. Nevertheless, I learned a few things. I continue to read voluminously and with great joy.

Sometimes, however, I felt that the words got in the way of my thought, and I sought an open silence. At such moments, I listened to and took great comfort in orchestral music. My engagement with literature led me to entertain some questions about the music to which I attended. But even in my unfocused and casual consideration, I sensed the existence of Thoreau's bottomless pond into which my imagination might freely plunge. Thoreau said, "While men believed in the infinite, some ponds will be thought to be bottomless." In the music—and especially that of Ludwig van Beethoven—I began to sense the presence of the infinite. In this music, no words obstructed my plunge. In the music, I swam in emotion until an idea surfaced, and I grasped onto it for buoyancy. Steeped in the music, I felt immersed in the immeasurable, and I enjoyed the opportunity to find some ballast.

In the symphony, I found a large creative work comprised of four separate movements each written in a distinctive musical form. These separate and different structures seemed to be all necessary to the integrity of the voice of the whole work, though, indeed, any single movement might be heard in isolation, as sometimes disappointingly occurs on Public Radio stations where time is a factor. I speculated about what made the whole symphony greater and different than the sum of its parts. How was it possible, I wondered, to understand meaning in the symphony when there were no words from which to make meaning? When Hector Berlioz, in his essay on Beethoven, mentioned theme, he referred to the particular presentation and elaboration of a musical melody and not to the *meaning* of the work as a whole or to the meaning of even the particular movement he analyzed. He notes that in Beethoven's Eighth Symphony, for example, the first movement had two themes, both gentle and peaceful in character.

But Berlioz knew there was more to the symphony than its musical themes. Speaking specifically of Beethoven's symphonies, Berlioz commented, "Only at rare intervals does our French public experience the keen and incandescent emotion that the art of music can generate; but when its emotions are truly stirred, nothing can equal its gratitude for the artist who caused this, whoever he may be." Emotions are felt and words are understood, the former experienced viscerally and the latter intellectually. But emotions are always *about* something. The music of the symphony possessed ideas although the piece itself did not define a precise intellectual content. Beethoven's symphonies were not program music that plotted some linear story, and I appreciated that when I listened to Beethoven it was not for the linguistic meanings I had been trained to discover and interpret in works of literature. Rather, the music of Beethoven inspired stirring emotions that allowed me to *explore* ideas that were inspired by, but not embedded in, the music itself. Beethoven's themes allowed the ideas to develop, and the development of the movements explored the ideas in separate, distinct but linked structures.

In my attempt to understand the form, I studied the origins of the symphony and its historical evolution. The *Grove Musical Dictionary* says, "the genre's identity rests in part upon external criteria of size and structure: composers consistently designated as a symphony a work for a medium — or large — sized orchestra, usually consisting of three, four, or five movements." But this definition gave me little insight into the content of the symphony. I read that like much instrumental music, the symphony was early considered mere entertainment, but in the work of Franz Joseph Haydn, Wolfgang Amadeus Mozart and Beethoven, the symphony "emerged as an institutional projection of the beliefs and aspirations of composers, performers and audiences alike." The work of these composers transformed the notion of music from mere background accompaniment into a medium that could evoke images and emotions that transcended the world of sound. In the work of these composers, music became an intellectual as well as an emotional, even aesthetic experience.

The symphony was an intellectual creation meant to address the emotions through the medium of sound. Having some issues to expose and develop, I desired to approximate in language my experience of Beethoven's music. This present work is the result of my effort.

Symphony #1 was begun in the spring of 2005 as brief sketches that I composed and placed on my blog. I had developed *Of Clay and Wattles Made* as a forum where I might be able to think aloud, even publically, about items and issues that concerned me in my daily life. About his book of essays Montaigne says, "Thus, reader, I am myself the matter of my book; you would be unreasonable to spend your leisure on so frivolous and vain a subject." So was it with my blog.

Despite his disclaimer, I am certain Montaigne hoped that others would read his work. He did, after all, publish his manuscript in several editions! And for me, the blog was a forum for my random thoughts. I will never know to what extent anyone ever read or reads my work. But over the past six years, I have regularly maintained the blog and trust that others occasionally have discovered my ruminations as they explored the world-wide web.

Over these same years, I began to recognize themes in my writing to which I kept returning. They were the themes that I think had drawn me originally to the works of Bob Dylan, Henry David Thoreau, Philip Roth . . . and presently to that of Ludwig van Beethoven. Music producer and writer Maynard Solomon writes of Beethoven's 3rd Symphony: "A unique characteristic of the *Eroica* symphony—and of its heroic successors—is the incorporation into musical form of death, destructiveness, anxiety, and aggression, as terrors to be transcended within the work of art itself." Such were the themes that had come to inhabit my consciousness and more recently, my intellectual work. I have lived in troubled and troubling times. I age with more and less grace. I have not always fared so well, though I remain fully aware that I have much for which to give thanks. As Dylan, Thoreau and Roth provided me some insight into myself and my world through the medium of language constructed and arranged in beautiful forms, so, too, did Beethoven deepen my experience in the world through non-linguistic means. Solomon says: "Beethoven's music does not merely express man's capacity to endure or even to resist suffering—his sonata cycles continue to project—on a vastly magnified scale—the essential features of high comedy: happy endings, joyful reconciliations, victories won and tragedy effaced." These expressions and projections, I believe, are what drew me to Beethoven's work, even as I think they had drawn me originally to literature.

My present passion for the music—and particularly the symphonies—of Ludwig van Beethoven followed a year of daily listening to Bob Dylan's *Modern Times* album, a work that portrayed a world breaking up and in despair, and yet a world from which joy may be ephemerally wrung. I return regularly to the novels of Philip Roth and find myself particularly drawn to American Pastoral, I Married a Communist, and *The Human Stain,* at the core of which lie what I have come to understand as the tragedy of the human condition. Thoreau has long been a mentor in my life, and I am never far from neither Walden nor Ktaadn.

Symphony #1 consists of four movements, each loosely modeled on a different musical form: *sonata allegro, marche funebre, scherzo,* and *theme and variations,* linked by the emotion with which I address the experiences of a life lived and celebrated. Though each movement can be read separately, the entire symphony is thematically linked and stands as an extended (and extensive) whole.

Symphony #1 begins not with birth nor ends in death, though these subjects run through the work; the symphony nevertheless presents the experience of a life - I am deeply into my sixties - in which beginnings and endings figure significantly. This life takes place on the pond's shores, but there are times when Walden's bottom may be sounded. Sometimes I think there is someone there, and other times, it's only me.

In the first movement, *sonata allegro,* I develop the theme of home-leavings and homecomings, occurrences that I think happen always amidst storm. The movement begins with a slow, elongated introduction that sets the outlines of the movement's theme: the conflicted and unsettled nature of the home that we must leave only to arrive still at home. Juxtaposing stories from Genesis and personal experience with a variety of scheduled reunions, I explore within the movement the contradictory nature of departing from and arriving home.

I am concerned with what it means about our lives when we choose to leave home and then to discover home out in the world. The paradoxical nature of this experience is expressed in metonymic patterns exploring scriptural and autobiographical instances of home leavings and arrivals. This movement also introduces themes that will appear throughout the symphony: relationships, family, memory, desire, and death.

The second movement, the *marche funebre*, centers on the funerals of three very different deaths and explores the idea of death from the perspective of the burial traditions of Judaism. In this movement, I consider what these practices of death suggest to us about life. Borrowing the rhythms of the second movements of Beethoven's 3rd and 7th symphony, the movement represents a slow march to and from the grave.

The theme of the third movement—the *scherzo*, (in Italian scherzo means joke)—looks with a jaundiced eye at my daily world. I am concerned in this movement with the jokes that are told as a strategy for managing the private and public policies about which we read in our newspapers and by which we daily live. Through the joke, I explore how the absurd world arrives at my house and occupies my consciousness. And I begin with the ancient story of Balaam and Balak, for I find there an early comic portrayal of the consequences of human hubris and greed that will be again depicted in the hilarious madness in the movies of the Marx Brothers. The insistence in the latter that there is no sanity clause is prefigured in Balaam's frustrated attempts to accomplish anything that he has with serious intent set out to do. He is transformed into a buffoon by his efforts.

Specifically, the theme of this third movement is presented at the outset: *a story is told.* Punctuated by jokes and commentary, the movement develops with the stories we tell as a result of the stories we are told. As Freud suggests, the joke provides us the "ability to provide pleasure against the objections raised by criticism that would put an end to pleasure." In this chapter, I employ the joke to address some of the absurdities of our present time that are too, too evident in our society, our politics, newspapers and news programs, and in the misplaced critique of our educational system.

In the fourth and final movement, I have written a celebration of life and of hope. Inspired by the final movement of Beethoven's 7th Symphony, I have attempted to explore and elaborate the idea of the sublime as the experience of immanent transcendence available always in our daily lives. The Rabbis' ability to find presence in absence seemed to me a wonderful strategy for dealing with life outside of Eden. I wanted to close my symphony with a sense of joy, triumph and celebration. The sublime is available to us, but we must be open to its appearance. Sometimes we think we are all alone, but at other times, we know someone else is there. The symphony ends, of course, in song, one that speaks to the reality of our condition and to strategies we can enact not only to accept but to thrive within it. This may not be the best of all possible worlds, but it is the only world we possess.

In his book *The Ninth: Beethoven and the World in 1824*, Harvey Sachs recounts the story of a composer who arises from his piano having played a recent composition for a small, intimate audience. "Ah, how beautiful," a guest comments, "and what does it mean?"

The composer nods, returns to the piano, and plays the piece again.

Music means itself. Jacques Barzun has said, " . . . it is plain that the composer can use sounds to set off a particular stirring within us. But the stirring is nameless, so that if it does not accompany the words of a text and yet we want to refer to it, we have to make up some analogy." Such is the hope that I have for Symphony #1: it may not contain truth, or even possess meaning, but it does explore thoughts and ideas that have consumed my life for many years now. In four movements, I have attempted to sound those themes in hopes that they might set off a stirring in the reader.

TO TIME AND PLACE...

FIRST MOVEMENT
Sonata Allegro

/agitato/ Late at night and during the early summer months out here in the Midwest, roiling thunderstorms draw us from our sleep, and we—the family—shudder in our beds in astonishment and dread. Vague rumblings move into our dreams, the drum tuning at the rear of the concert stage. Within our sleep, we anticipate the violent assault we have learned from experience that the muted rolls portend. Though the storm remains miles away, the increasingly insistent thunder takes on the irregular beat of an orchestra comprised of deep tympani drums tuned to diminished fifths. This primeval symphony of percussion beats into the most intimate body recesses. We know what it portends and lie tremblingly awake in our beds, hopelessly hoping the storm will keep its distance. In this first movement of the storm, through the curtainless windows we see the lightning flicker in the near distance, as a bulb flashing down, though we cannot yet hear the lightning's sharp, cracking sound. Inevitably, as the storm moves closer, razor-sharp bolts will slice cleanly through the skies toward our rooftops. The awakened and now-frightened children climb into my bed, and we all slip further under the light cotton blanket in vain hope of falling back to sleep. Like a cry in the night, the storm calls us awake.

As the storm nears, the thunder intensifies in shattering, shuddering decibels and reaches into the house walls, shaking us who already quake in our beds. Lightning cracks the sky with the sound of new wood torn and splintered. We lie in our beds certain that one of the thunderclaps will rip in two our flimsy, solitary home atop the hill and expose us naked to the brutal physical assault of the violent storm.

Our beds feel no longer safe, and we rise from them to stand wide-eyed at the window as if as witnesses we can tame the assault. The dark shapes of standing tall trees whipped by the violent winds snap back and forth, and I expect to see one of them go flying, uprooted and groundless past our window, like Miss Gulch pedaling steadily on her bicycle in the midst of the twister. Thunder rolls incessantly and now fills the air with the sound of a thousand tympani drums. The lightning, in strobe-like bursts, flashes in split-second intervals. Rain lashes the ground and the roof and our windows in unsteady but persistent rhythms. It is demanding attention and even entrance. The rain's rhythmic drumming is in counterpoint to the thunder and lightning, and altogether it makes an unholy sound out of which I expect monsters to rise. I think of Mussorgsky's "A Night on Bald Mountain," but it is late June and not All Hallow's Eve, and this isn't recorded music but real nature threatening. Wrapped in the storm, we have become the storm. Home is not where we want to be, but it is where we are; home does not feel safe, and yet it is all the safety we have.

[eroico] Sometimes the storm insists that I come out my front door and confront it, even if I experience its threat in the physical safety of my living room sitting upright before the fire place in my favorite cushioned wing chair. Such is the storm that rages throughout Beethoven's Fifth Symphony. "Thus, fate knocks at the door," and this storm, fate's emissary, demands that I acknowledge its presence and face it. In my listening I am emotionally pulled out of the safety of my home by the summons of its call. Why I follow baffles me; perhaps I mean to confront the fierce tempest, to accept its challenge and challenge myself. Perhaps I am drawn by the insistence of the taunt. Perhaps I am too afraid to refuse its dare. The tensions implicit in the demand of the summons—ta-ta-ta-TA—the short bursts of eighth notes followed by a lowered, half-note held by a *fermata*, threaten my calm and security. Its persistent assertion disturbs my rest, and my home is no refuge. During this first movement, the storm steals away my breath; I find no safety from it, know no place to hide, and yet I am irresistibly drawn outside by its insistence and power and violence. I stand vulnerable outside of the door.

I am offered some respite from the onslaught by the symphony's second movement, to be played, Beethoven insists, *andante con moto* (slowly with *motion*). It is a somewhat long and even untroubled respite from the storm, though in this calm I remain anxiously aware of the storm's return, and I take deep breaths. The melodies here are lyrical, almost triumphant, and I feel almost safe; I hope the struggle is over, but I sense it is not. Indeed, the storm has not at all dissipated, and this illusory calm does not resolve into any praise to God as at the end of the 'storm' in Beethoven's 6th Symphony. Rather, what might have been a peaceful resolution is transformed into a defiant stance by the insistent tensions of the cellos and basses. The night here is now dark, and though at home I am not at home. I may be bloodied, but I insist unbowed.

And with the opening bars of the Third Movement, with the threatening rumbling of the basses and a reprise of the opening insistent and portentous four-note summons voiced first in the horns and then the strings, the storm returns in full fury, and I am now out too far to find shelter to protect me from the onslaught. I am on my own and the only resource at my disposal; I am not at ease. The storm beats at me, and in the final moments of the Third Movement that begin with the ominous sound of the tympani drums, a furious assault by the menacing storm begins. The violins enter and churn portentously in tension with the tonic key; they rise slowly in pitch and intensity and volume, as if waiting an order for the final attack, and move anxiously, even tauntingly about in uncertain and irregular melodies. The music fights with itself, gathering forces, its power bent on destruction. The violins continue to struggle upwards, but then shift slowly yet steadily away from conflict and discordance until in the final swirlings the strings reach the tonic key of C major, and there, joined by the entire orchestra, the threatening storm is transformed into a moment of triumph, and in a glorious resolution, the entire orchestra propels me seamlessly into the exultant opening chords of the magnificent fourth movement.

The storm menaces still in this final movement, but I know I have prevailed. Whenever now it threatens, its tensions resolve into triumph. I have become stronger than the storm which continues to rage. I am no longer cowed. I have been battered and scathed, but *this* storm *for now* has been overcome. The last measures of Beethoven's Fifth Symphony are filled with triumph: twenty-nine out of the final forty-one measures are tonic C major chords; I recall that I began this struggle in the key of C minor and have now come through into the major. And the final moments in this symphony speak ebulliently. In the symphony's final measure, the entire orchestra plays the plain and simple C notes; no tension or dissonant element remains anywhere. I have not only withstood the storm, but transformed it into my triumph. I am stronger now, and I am home.

≈

/animato/ Sometimes we are already outside when the storm arrives, and though we seek shelter from it, we are not able to avoid its assault. Though this particular storm threatens, there is more *sturm* than *drang* in its rage. It leaves us soaked but fundamentally unchallenged. This is the storm that blows Dorothy right out of Kansas and into Oz. "It's a twister, it's a twister," the farm hand calls, and on the horizon, the dark swirling funnel cloud reaches from earth to heaven blowing away everything in its path and sending it hurtling uncontrollably through the air. The tornado passes dangerously close to Dorothy as she seeks shelter from the storm, and the wind's force violently blows the windows out where she stands calling for Auntie Em and Uncle Henry who already cower in the shelter under the home. One of those window frames knocks Dorothy unconscious and sends her dreaming. In that dream, she and her house land somewhere over the rainbow in the Technicolor Oz. "I have a feeling," Dorothy says, "we're not in Kansas anymore." The storm has blown her far from home.

But in fact, I think, Dorothy remains stolidly in black and white Kansas. Everyone from her home still exists in Oz, albeit in slightly altered form, and though to the viewer each is recognizable, they do not seem to be familiar to Dorothy. She must learn that home is the ultimate goal. Later, it will seem that she had, indeed, recognized in Oz the people she knew back in Kansas. Seemingly blown away by the storm, Dorothy learns that her dream of a better life over the rainbow, a childish dream heard once in a lullaby, is an illusion. The delight for which she wished over the rainbow she learns can really only be realized here at home. Perfection exists only here, at home. Indeed, it is only the nasty Miss Gulch, the prototype for the wicked witch, who is missing at the film's end. The witch has been melted. Dorothy's storm illusorily blew all the evils of her home away but in fact, touched nothing at all and left everything exactly as it had been before the tornado struck. Dorothy accepts unqualifiedly the version of home offered by the man behind the curtain and by Glinda, the Witch of the East. "There's no place like home," Dorothy continues to intone. I am not certain what she means by that, but I suspect that it is a greater illusion than her fantasy of a place "over the rainbow."

/patetico/ Finally, there is the storm Walter Benjamin describes in his "Theses on the Philosophy of History." He says, "A Klee painting named 'Angelus Novus' shows an angel looking as though he is about to move away from something he is fixedly contemplating. His eyes are staring, his mouth is open, his wings are spread. This is how one pictures the angel of history. His face is turned toward the past. Where we perceive a chain of events, he sees one single catastrophe that keeps piling wreckage and hurls it in front of his feet. The angel would like to stay, awaken the dead, and make whole what has been smashed. But a storm is blowing in from Paradise; it has got caught in his wings with such violence that the angel can no longer close them. The storm irresistibly propels him into the future to which his back is turned, while the pile of debris before him grows skyward. This storm is what we call progress."

This storm is what we call progress, but it is a delusion. The face of Benjamin's Angel is turned toward the past. The angel, looking back, sees not a series of events, but one huge catastrophe that keeps piling "wreckage upon wreckage" at his feet. To the angel, history is not some forward progress, effected in fits and starts and in botched beginnings and failed means; rather, history is one disastrous and calamitous blunder piled atop another. The angel would love to stay and to make whole what has been broken, but "a storm blows from Paradise," and that storm irresistibly propels the angel, head turned toward the past, into a future the angel cannot see. This storm, says Benjamin, is called progress, but it is some violent and uncontrollable force blowing us blindly into an unseen future, even while we stare uncomprehendingly at the shards of a broken past that we would, but cannot, repair. We are blown forward by the storm into a future we cannot know or even control, as we are compelled (is it by the storm, I wonder?) to look back on a past we cannot understand. Our blind and will-less entry into that future blown by the storm called progress is hardly a sign of advancement, however, though our movement appears to us as forward. This storm, unlike that which blows Dorothy out of Kansas and into the parallel Oz, blows us willy-nilly into a future that we cannot see. Rather it is the past on which our eyes are fixed, though that past remains incomprehensible to us. Benjamin's angel can neither repair the past nor control the future. Home is the catastrophe to which the idea of return offers illusory hope. But the storm of progress prevents that return. This storm of progress that cannot be controlled or paused blows the angel—and us—forward into some unknown future though our eyes remain fixed on the catastrophe that is the past. Here, the home to which we go is forever unseen, but the home from which we go is forever in view as disaster.

⫽

/grazioso/ I've been thinking about home-leavings and homecomings. For some years now, I have regularly experienced what I have come to call 'homecoming dreams.' In each of them, I am out in the world somewhere, doing something, trying to get home, but in the dream I find it frustratingly impossible to get there. I am kept from home sometimes by circumstances out in the world, and sometimes, I am obstructed by my own physical failures. In the dream, I cannot find my way home, or for some reason, I am incapable of moving towards it. I become agitated and alarmed, and despite all of my efforts and longing, I realize no progress and remain, alas, frustratingly in a form of exile. Though I long to arrive home, I have no facility or power to get there. When I thankfully awaken, my heart beats furiously and I am out of breath. I feel distressed yet relieved to discover myself safe and in my own bed. Though I awaken from the dream always at 'home,' I am troubled by the recurrence of this dream in which I cannot get home even when I am already there.

In my life, I have never been homeless. Awake now, in moments of reflective tranquility, I wonder where and what is the dream home to which I have such desire, yet no capacity, to return. This home is not distinguished by specific place or location. In my dreams, I think, home is an amalgam of the places I have called home. Nor is this home identified consistently with any precise constellation of people from a specific period in my life. *When* did I live in the home from which I am kept now away. And I wonder whether *this home* to which in the dream I want to return is actually *that home* toward which I head never to arrive while I am yet awake.

There are many ways to leave home, and perhaps only one way to remain there.

≠

I come out here to my office cabin — Walden — in the now-cold early mornings from a very warm bed in an environmentally inefficient house. It is an older residence, and the structure leaks in so many places that the children complain we might as well live out of doors. In the winters, the often harsh elements enter through many cracks, and the children defiantly refuse to remove their outer coats when they enter. One year, we installed a gas fireplace that produces not a little heat in the downstairs, and each early morning before I leave by the back door, I ignite the fire to warm the room by pushing a button on a remote control device. During one particularly cold morning that first winter, one daughter sat too close to the fire and while eating her breakfast, melted the back of her costly coat. Of course, she blamed me for the mishap, and that week, she purchased a much warmer, less flammable, and far more expensive North Face full-length jacket. Over the years, we've learned a greater sense of caution, and in our homes, breakfast from December through April is almost traditionally eaten seated — now coatless — before the fire. Nevertheless, despite the blustery weather in here, I am always a bit loathe to leave this windy place, especially in the early morning darkness.

At 5:30 a.m., the air is crisply frigid, and lately, the cloudless black sky has been sharply clear. The stars do not any longer twinkle, but they do rest steadily in the skies, setting limits to how far into the universe I can see. I do not see very far at all, in fact. The astrophysicists tell me that the universe is expanding and may do so forever, though they do not seem to know into what it expands. Perhaps into what the universe expands accords with my concept of God, or even my hope for immortality. I am not comforted by the former or confident in the latter. As long as the stars are visible, however, I feel securely cloaked against the voids. A cloudy night can often disrupt my ease. Philip Roth writes in Everyman that the stars remind him of imminent death, but it is a very unhappy book, and although I must be included in the 'everyman' category, I am not yet that sorrowful. Perhaps it is the stars' twinkling that leads Roth to liken them to death, but my steady stars merely set limits within which I think I can live. The fault is never in the stars, anyway, but in myself, methinks.

I step out of the door and away from the house, carrying a

precariously full mug of coffee, my cell phone, and whatever books I think necessary and can physically manage to bear. I learned long ago not to travel anywhere without an abundance of reading materials suitable for the variety of situations in which I might find myself— books in multiple genres, newspapers, journals—and I have stayed obsessively true to that practice. By the rule, I travel heavy. I do speculate amusedly as I step through the door about when it was I learned to carry my cell phone, and I wonder who might ring me up at 5:30am. But actually, I know the answer to this latter question: one of the children from a different time zone or an announcement of a death. From somewhere, E.T. calls home. And I have become it.

I move cautiously down the three steps that lead away from the house and into the yard; a motion-sensor light above the rear door of the house flashes on to guide my way, and I start the short passage of fifty yards across the lawn toward Walden which sits not fifty yards northeast of the house, a cabin constructed on the outskirts of some woods, but not in them like Thoreau's. There is no pond out here, though in the spring, melting snow and fertile rains produce a verita- ble marshland through which I step armored in my high Wellington boots. When I move within twenty feet of the entrance, the second motion sensor light above the cabin door blazes on and lights this fool along the dusty path. Forward and backward my way is now illu- mined. It *is* better to light a candle than curse the darkness, though at times the lit candle produces too much glare. The walk out here is not very long, and over the years, I have worn a well-beaten path to the door. In the summers, the way is marked by grass trodden to a lighter shade of pale, and in the winters, the frozen path on which I walk lies like a shallow ditch cut between steep banks of snow. I try not to spill too much coffee from the too-filled mug, and after a few more healthy and anxious strides, I arrive at the cabin a bit chilled but secure, place the mug gently atop the neat wooden shelf my dear comrade has fashioned outside the entry door for just such moments, turn the knob and enter. The anticipation of the elixir speeds my way. I choose to wait until I am seated before the open computer screen to taste the day's brew, and so the anticipation of the coffee and the writing leads me on. I open the door and step in out of the cold to the warmth. I move out of the light and into the dark. Both outdoor lamps extinguish. The night is dark, and I am far from home.

Though perhaps not far enough. Leaving home is more than a physical parting, and though I close the door to the cabin, there yet remains too many places of ingress. I come out here as a means to get away from in there; here, I do things that have become impossible to accomplish there. And yet, out here, I often feel drawn back into the house. In this compulsion, I have become the nightmare version of my dreams. Out here, I obsess about things that I have cautioned those in there to let go; here, I pile up too many books and papers to read that I have carried from there; out here, I postpone writing projects and distract myself with the needs and desires and insecurities and inadequacies I cannot leave behind in there; here, I leak without cease though certainly with honest cause. I sweep the floor with too much energy and abandon, and dust the desks with a fury. I pick at too many of the leftovers. Out here, there are, indeed, too many places of ingress.

I get up from my chair and move to the door, and I see nothing through the dimness. The house remains very dark and no one moves, not even the mouse. But the house pulls me toward it nonetheless. Or is it I that push towards the house?

I am considering that 'letting go' may be one of the primary and steady processes of living. In the colloquial, 'letting go' refers to losing one's self to a sense of abandonment—to release the repressed self to spontaneity, to unself-consciousness, and even to joy. Alcohol and drugs are aids to this letting go, and I suspect good sex results from it. But to completely let go is to be left without roots, and like a balloon, drift upwards blown about by even the slightest breeze. Letting go without a reconnecting means to be always without family, and so I consider that to let go is also to lose primary connection. Leaving home is letting go, and I am beginning to suspect that we never stop leaving home, but we never quite arrive there either. Perhaps letting go is a state of equilibrium.

I am referring to the letting go of roles that tie me to ways of being that are no longer life-giving for either myself or those with whom I live. For example, I can no longer be the same father to the nineteen-year-old as I was to the ten-year-old. When I try to be so, I engage in behaviors and emotions no longer appropriate to the present and entrap myself in positions and situations no longer productive for growth and living. Spinoza knew that such emotions led to states of human bondage. Refusing to let go, I insist on using scripts for the wrong play. I speak beautiful lines in improper settings. I enslave myself and my daughters.

And neither can the nineteen-year-old be the same sister to the fourteen-year-old as the fourteen-year-old was to the nine-year-old. Indeed, very often she can't even be the same sister today as she was yesterday because today, so much has changed from then. She has to let go. But it is so hard to do so, especially if there was so much reward in yesterday's relationship. The letting go acknowledges that what yesterday offered as a satisfying reward is today unhealthy dependency. Letting go makes us free.

And so, we have to learn how to 'let go' of the singular nature of the relationship and the behaviors we have attached to it, though these behaviors and emotions may be stored and readily available for a time when they might again be appropriate, though that moment might not ever again occur or even be recognized when it does. I will again misbehave. Home is what I must leave in order to go anywhere though never to arrive. Home is from where I depart from those whom I know and go to those whom I will leave.

/*trionfante*/ Once, I headed home for the Thanksgiving holiday. Returning to family returned me to unacknowledged—repressed—parts of myself, with no opportunity or companionship to manage these conflicts because everyone present had already their assigned role and place in my scripted drama. At these festivities, all these feelings and attitudes erupted like Vesuvius, and like the lava that flowed from the volcano and immobilized Pompeii, these feelings and memories erupted to flow and freeze and smother the present. At these events, I returned to the home in which I was raised and returned again to the boy whose man I have become. I think as long as memories stay buried, they do not change—but then, the behaviors built on those memories don't change either. Perseveration. Compulsive obsessions. Re-enactments with no consciousness of the original act. Let's go. (They do not move). I leave home and try to move on but I am called back. I do not move. I go home because I think I have moved on. I do not move.

Freud notes that as long as the Pompeian artifact remained buried under the ash it remains also preserved, but once it is recovered in an archaeological dig, it is subject to decay. So with memories: when I do not think upon them, they remain untouched, but as soon as they are uncovered, these memories are subject to the natural effects of the present, and then they become, if not inaccurate, then certainly unreliable. These buried memories of home affect the lay of the land, but unearthed, they lose their relationship to the earth they helped shaped and thus, lose their connection to terra firma. What hope for self-awareness and insight do memories offer except as portents for the present and indications for the future? I've never been very fond of nostalgia, a term I have too long defined as a longing for an event or emotion that never truly occurred. Nostalgia derives from decayed memory and rests upon the bedrock of regret. I think that throughout his life, my father lived in nostalgia and consequently in regret, torn between the wished-for past and the unsatisfying present. He moved nowhere exhaustingly. He would too often say, "If I knew then what I know now, I'd be a rich man today!" Then he would shake his head with sorrow, and stare through me toward some distant past. What I think he meant was that if only he knew the end at the beginning, then the end at which he had arrived would have been different. For him, life was all ends and not means, and the home from which he left every day was always a disappointment when he returned to it. He never knew or had enough, and he was always unhappy.

When I moved away from home, with effort, I learned a different path. I learned with some discomfort and dis-ease to let go. I began to run long distances and discovered that engaging in running had everything to do with means and nothing about ends. At the end of every six, or ten, or twenty mile run, I realized that I had not finished, and that tomorrow, I would again be out running on the roads. I never intended to win the race, though I had committed myself never to finish last. Every run was part of the means, and there was no end in sight. I would always run and never arrive, never look back, and never see too far ahead. And that was all right with me. Every run was a new day, and every day a new run.

To accompany myself, I listened first to a radio where the soundtrack was someone else's design, and then, when they became available, I bought myself an iPod with which I could control the musical accompaniment to my efforts. One evening, I loaded several dozen songs onto the device in anticipation of a ten mile run, and I set the controls on this wonder-toy to 'shuffle.' The songs would now come up in no set order, but rather, occur according to some algorithm I would never comprehend. I had much to think about over the distances as I ran from home. On that day in May, on my father's Yahrzeit, I thought about his life and his regret.

There were two particular and serendipitous moments that reinforced what I believe I had been learning. The thought of my father set the theme on this run, and what I heard on the soundtrack gave that theme elaboration. Moment One at mile one occurred during Dylan's song from *The Basement Tapes*, "Nothing Was Delivered:" "Nothing is better, nothing is best/Take heed of this and get plenty rest." I am certain this was not a political statement of resignation and despair, but an acknowledgment that life is best lived satisfied and that the grasping and competitive nature of society opposes achieving peace and fulfillment. Dylan's was not a retreat from the struggle, but an assertion of resistance to the desperation that drives acquisitiveness in the United States. No regrets here, and no resignation either. It is life and life only, and life is to be lived. In running from home, I think I'd been trying to learn this so that I could find home. I am still running.

And there occurred a second moment during the eighth mile. It was during "Ramble On Rose," one of my favorite songs of the Grateful Dead. This is what *they* sang, and *I* heard: "The grass ain't greener, the wine ain't sweeter, either side of the hill." Ram Dass had urged us to be here now, but the Dead told me why. Jack Nicholson wondered in despair, "What if this is as good as it gets," but the Dead never gave this idea a second thought. It never gets any better, and it never gets any worse. Life just is, and there is nothing either good or bad but thinking makes it so. There is joy in the present, and the wine we've got now might be drunk with some pleasure because this is as good as it gets. And I am happy for that.

Nostalgia is exactly the opposite emotion. It regrets everything, because nothing ever compares to the invention of reality. What exists always pales next to the imaginative reconstruction of an imagined paradisiacal moment in some illusory and therefore, elusive, past. Here, nostalgia seeks a return to a place that never existed; in nostalgia lays a regret of everything in the present and the real. There is for the nostalgic no entrance to the castle. Nostalgia tries to return me to that which never existed, beating against the current and borne back ceaselessly into the past. Nostalgia sends me home to defeat.

/*affetuoso*/ Home is what I must leave in order to go anywhere but never to arrive. Home is from where I depart from those whom I know to go to those whom I will leave. Life is constant movement. Dylan says, "Everybody's moving, if they ain't already there, everybody's got to move somewhere." We start moving away from home, and then continue on until we get there. But where 'there' remains unknown, that unknown bourn from which no traveler returns does, indeed, trouble many a will. On one of his trips from home, Thoreau traveled to explore the Maine Woods. On the top of Mt. Ktaadn, Thoreau discovered a wildness he could not tolerate. At Ktaadn's peak "inhuman Nature" says to humankind, 'I cannot pity nor fondle thee here, but forever relentlessly drive thee hence to where I *am* kind. Why seek me where I have not called thee, and then complain because you find me but a stepmother? Should thou freeze or starve, or shudder thy life away, here is no shrine nor altar, nor any access to my ear'." Away is not always better than home. Indeed, Thoreau had discovered that he had travelled too, too far from home and experienced alarm. Descending Ktaadn, Thoreau returned home to Concord, though I think that on his return he might have discovered home had changed. Walden Woods had become wilderness enough for him.

Home is what I must leave in order to go anywhere but never to arrive. Home is from where I depart from those whom I know and go to those whom I will leave. Hamlet says that he might be bounded in a nutshell but that he has bad dreams, and these would travel with him wherever he traveled. He might never leave home, in fact. The trouble with traveling from home, of course, is that I have to take myself and families of origin and choice along with me. Too often I carry home on my back as my burden, and though it is not visible, it yet weighs heavily on my mobility. But let me change the metaphor: The powerful gravitational pull of home requires a considerable thrust to achieve release, and then we have to jettison the engine that effected our breaking free of this force in order to continue our movement outwards. Perhaps Desire is the propulsion that sends us out from home. But Desire is known only by what it seeks and not for itself. I only know that when I seek, I follow my Desire; I know when my Desire achieves some fulfillment, but I never know my desire. Maybe what traveling from home is all about is following distance and learning its limits. We leave home to find home and never to arrive.

But how far must one go to say one has left home? Kafka traveled remarkable distances in his writing. He never physically left home, but can it be said that he ever existed there at all? I recall once reading that during meals, Kafka chewed every mouthful one hundred times. I do not think he could have spoken much during meals. To whom in his home was he ever present? Was he ever home, or was he always leaving? Where was he going, and whom did he have to meet? Where was he heading, and when did he arrive? I am interested in home-leavings and homecomings, trying to avoid mistaking paradise for that home across the road. I wonder about my Desire. How does this blue-eyed son meet anyone?

I've got a few questions.

A tale is told: A man tormented by doubts about the meaning of life and the nature of truth decided to make a pilgrimage to the home of the rabbi known as the wisest man in the entire country. And so the man packed whatever possessions he thought he might require for this journey into his car, said goodbye to his family and friends, and drove off on a very long and exhausting drive. Finally, he arrived at the doorstep of the Rabbi, but when he begged for admission, he was refused. "The Rabbi has been working on a particular problem for years and to see him one has to make an appointment a long time in advance and have good cause. Besides, we do not know you. I'm sorry, you cannot see the Rabbi." And so the man was sent away very disappointed. But he was not vanquished.

The next day, he returned and again asked for a meeting with the Rabbi for just one hour, this time offering a large sum of money. The man had been very successful in business. But the disciples laughed contemptuously and again showed the man the door.

On the third day, the man avoided the front door altogether, but went around to the rear of the house, and when all seemed quiet, he climbed in like a common thief through the window. He hid himself in a closet but left the door open just a crack so that he might observe the activities in the house. He saw right away that one door not far down the hall remained slightly ajar, and from inside, he could hear the Rabbi studying, turning pages, mumbling some inaudible words seemingly in conversation with someone not readily observable to the man hidden in the closet. At times the Rabbi seemed to hum joyously a short *niggun*. At other times, the man heard the Rabbi moan as if in some kind of distress.

The man stealthily moved out of the closet and toward the door to the Rabbi's room. Holding the knob in his right hand, he placed his left hand on the weathered wood for balance, and pushed gently on the door. It opened without a creak, and there, with his back to the door at his desk, sat the Rabbi dwarfed by the mountains of books piled on all sides of him, hunched at the moment over one specific book open wide before him.

"Rabbi," the man whispered, leaning his head through the crack in the door. But of course, the Rabbi was too immersed in his study to hear the man, and so he spoke a bit louder. "Rabbi, excuse me, please." And this time, the old man heard the imprecation, and he turned and looked toward the door. For about a minute, the Rabbi stared at the man, and then he motioned with his arm feebly for the man to enter.

"Why are you here? For what have you come?"

The man slowly entered the room. He held his hat in his hand. He said, "Rabbi, I have come a great distance with a question that has troubled me greatly. I know that you are the wisest of men, and have studied many of the great books, and I was hoping that you could offer me an answer to my question. I have been so sorely troubled."

The Rabbi looked at him silently for another minute. At last, he said quietly, "Well, what is the question?"

"Rabbi," the man started almost in sobs, "I want to be a good person and always do the right thing. Tell me, please, what is the Truth? How should I live?"

The Rabbi got slowly up out of his chair, walked over to the man and looked him directly in the eyes. And then he slapped the man across the face.

Well, the man was terribly upset and left the room blinded by his humiliation and his tears. He headed down the stairs and was there confronted by the Rabbi's students. They were alarmed that he had managed to elude their guard, but when they saw that the man wept so bitterly, they asked him to sit down at the table and drink a glass of tea until he became less agitated. At first, they remained silent, observing the bereft man as he cupped his shaking hands about the hot glass filled with the dark liquid. Finally, after several minutes, when he became somewhat calmer, one of the young men asked why he had been weeping. At first, he didn't speak, and the only noise in the room was that caused by the shifting of his glass on the table as he nervously spun it about, and the anguished sounds of his heart-broken sighs. He pulled a handkerchief from his pocket and blew his nose, and then, stuffing the handkerchief back into his pocket, he took a deep breath and staring down at the table, narrated what had occurred in the Rabbi's study. When he had finished, he looked up and around at the students about him.

"Why," he asked, "why did the Rabbi treat me like that? Why did the Rabbi slap me?" he demanded. "I only wanted him to tell me by what Truth I should live?

Of course, the men and women about the table were puzzled as well; they knew their rebbe as the most gentle of men who treated everyone with the utmost kindness.

For a while there was silence, and then a thin and pale young man standing behind the man at the table spoke up. "Ah," he said quietly, "the Rabbi slapped you so that you would learn never to trade a good question for an answer."

The question implies an unknown, a sense of mystery. "Come Watson, the game's afoot!" There is an excitement in the question, and perhaps our society has lost its delight in the mystery, magic and enchantment replete in the question. Questions open the world, and answers close it down. Questions inspire movement, but answers render further movement unnecessary. Questions are the enemies of falseness, and the answer falsely promises fulfillment. We are told that when the genome project is complete then we will know everything there is to know about the human being. All questions about human behavior will be finally answered. But I do not believe this at all. Will the map of my genes tell me know why I have fallen in love with one and not another, and then what I should do about it? Will it tell me why today for breakfast I want oatmeal and not eggs? How will knowing my genetic map improve my senses of humor or compassion? The question acknowledges that there is more to know, but the answer puts an end to curiosity. The question opens the world to speculation, and the answer closes it to wonder. There is nothing beyond the answer, but in the question the world is open to possibility. The question sends me out from home and into the world.

/sosenuoto/ Genesis is filled with dreams and home-leavings of the type about which I have been speaking. Home-leavings, indeed, seem to be the central theme of this first book of the Bible. I think of Adam and Eve, cast out of their home into the world to toil and to labor "all the days of your life," and destined to suffer pain in childbearing "until you return to the ground." But it is interesting to consider that having left their paradisiacal home *in* the Garden, they must now begin the endless work of repairing the world *outside* Eden. I wonder which might be considered their home, Eden or the other? Though following their expulsion Adam and Eve immediately have children, their place of residence—their home—is never described, as if the place itself holds no significance. Where did they live? They must, I assume, have created their own home by working the land. Perhaps having been banished from Eden, Adam and Eve never arrive home.

I think of Cain. Condemned to wander—we are told Cain settled in the land of Nod, East of Eden, but in Hebrew, the word *Nod* means wandering—and denied support from the soil in which he attempted to hide his brother's blood, Cain founds urban culture, itself characterized by a sense of rootlessness and transiency. In these early stories, Torah suggests that home is the place from which to depart to engage in the world; home must be transcended.

And I think of the patriarch, Abraham née Abram, who hears the word of God: "Go forth from your native land and from your father's house to the land that I will show you. I will make your name great, And you shall be a blessing, I will bless those who bless you and curse him that curses you; And all the families of the earth shall bless themselves by you." Home is what I must leave in order to go anywhere but never to arrive. Home is from where I depart from those whom I know and go to those whom I will leave.

Immediately, Abram departs his familial home and begins his life-long wanderings. Abraham's is a tale of great promise, but he is continually tested and sorely tried, and finally, never achieves the secure home he has left behind. One could say that Abraham's home-leaving is never followed by a homecoming. God continually promises Abraham that his offspring will be as plentiful as the dust of the earth and will occupy the land that God has promised, but it is only the Cave of Machpelach that Abraham will ever own and can call home, the tomb in which he will bury Sarah, née Sarai, and then be himself buried by his two sons, both of whom remain, with much justification, alienated from their father and their familial home. Though the land has been promised to him, Abraham never acquires the land. He is home, it might be said, only in the directive of his God: leave your home and go forth to a land that I will show you.

I wonder to what Abraham responds when he goes forth from his home? Traditionally, I have been taught that Abraham responds to the word of God, but I have always wondered how Abraham knew that it was God who spoke to him. Perhaps it *was* the word of God that Abraham heard, but I think that the word came not *to* but *out of* Abraham. Perhaps what Abraham followed was Desire. At some point content and even complacent, (Biblical ages are indistinct. I really don't know how old Abraham actually was when either this story took place or when he left home), Abraham becomes unsettled and anxious to roam. No sooner does he hear the directive, then he departs his home, taking with him that which he had already come to possess. "Abram took his wife Sarai, and his brother's son Lot, and all the wealth that they had amassed, and the persons that they had acquired in Haran; and they set out for the land of Canaan." The Rabbis say that those persons Abram took with him were those souls he had converted to the single God. They all left home together.

Abraham experienced a radical estrangement. One apocryphal story relates that Terah, Abraham's father, kept a shop that sold statues of the local idols. One day, Terah left Abraham to mind the store. Abraham smashed all of the idols but one. When his father returned and looked about, he was appalled to discover his entire inventory in irrecoverable pieces. Calling his son to him, Terah demanded to know what had occurred, and Abraham with mock ingenuousness reported that there had been some argument amongst the idols, and the largest idol had taken a stick and smashed all of the smaller idols.

Terah rebuked his son, saying that the idols were of clay and wood and could not become animate. Abraham asked how it was, then, that his father could believe in such lifeless gods.

This is a lovely story that I have heard told over my decades. I am certain I first learned it in Hebrew School. Indeed, I tell that story yet to my children, whenever the occasion might call for it. But I have never honestly known what it was that provoked Abraham's discomfort with the idols in the first place and led him to smash them. According to the midrash, no sooner did he break all of the idols then he received the word from God to leave his father's home. What thought provoked Abraham's act; what act provoked Abraham's thought? What provoked his leave taking? Perhaps he was motivated by the un-thought known: that inner impulse to make order and give structure to life that has for some reason and in some way become undone. Abraham responded to some question. Thousands of years later, Thoreau would note that one morning he awakened to an unanswered question. Perhaps it is that question that gives energy and direction to the day. Perhaps that is what energy is: the capacity to pursue the question. Perhaps Abraham responded to desire, the core of his being, and it appeared to him in the form of a directive. But really Abraham responded to a question. Home is what I must leave in order to go anywhere but never to arrive? Home is from where I depart from those whom I know and go to those whom I will leave?

Abraham was a seeker, a pursuer of unanswerable questions. His father's home had ceased to be his. What should I do? Where should I go? When Abraham broke the idols, it seems to be in response to his growing awareness that those idols once, but no longer, provided some anchor, and the security they once offered ceased to be effective. Those idols had once held the world in place, and smashing them left the world without meaning. Abraham went forth to make meaning. My intellectual hero, British literary theorist Terry Eagleton writes: "Whenever we stumble in literary works across a desire which starkly isolates a protagonist; renders him or her strange to themselves; expresses an ineluctable inner need; manifests an adamant refusal to compromise; invests itself in an object more precious than life itself; maroons a character between life and death, and finally bears him or her inexorably to the grave, we can be reasonably sure that we are in the presence of the Real." It is as if Eagleton were describing my Abraham. That Real is the formlessness that is Desire, and Desire, I think, is the foundation of Being. Abraham heads out not because he knows that which he seeks, but because he seeks an object in which his Desire might rest though his Desire might, even must, always remain unsatisfied.

What Abraham sought was inexpressible and unachievable; his heroism consists in his willingness to pursue Desire anyway. To pursue that Desire was the only way to become Abraham and to give sense to his world. But Abraham had to first leave home for an unknown and uncertain destination.

Abraham satisfies Desire by going out into the world. At home, he need neither risk nor offer anything of himself. Yet, once out into the world, one of his first responses is to serve it. Justice, justice thou shall pursue! Thus, the Torah recounts that while Abraham was sitting at the entrance to his tent in the heat of the day – three days after he had circumcised himself, Ishmael and all the people of his household – he lifted his eyes and saw three men standing near him. I imagine Abraham in great pain, recovering from a not inconsiderable surgical procedure. Yet, as soon as Abraham saw the travelers, "He ran from the entrance of the tent to greet them and, bowing to the ground, he said, 'My lords, if it please you, do not go on past your servant. Let a little water be brought; bathe your feet and recline under the tree. And let me fetch a morsel of bread that you may refresh yourselves; then go on.'" This going out to serve is almost always Abraham's first response, and when he does not follow this leaning, he suffers, as when he attempts to pass Sarah off as his sister in order to save his own life.

Perhaps it is justice that Abraham originally pursues, and it is in the pursuit that he arrives home. I like Abraham best when his Desire leads him to the pursuit of justice. This is exemplified to me in his pleadings for the cities of Sodom and Gomorrah. Beginning his bargaining with God from a standard of fifty righteous people who might be found in those wicked cities and for whom the cities might be saved, Abraham finally says, "Let not my Lord be annoyed and I will speak but once: What if ten would be found there?" It is this pursuit of justice, perhaps, that sends Abraham from his home and out into the world. It was perhaps this same Desire that led him to initially hear the word of God: Go, get you forth from your father's house and go to a land that I will show you. Abraham, you must leave home to satisfy your Desire, his Desire commands. It is, I think, to the land of Abraham's un-thought known that he travels to discover the objects with which he can create his home wherever he might find himself. It is not reality that Abraham seeks, for indeed, there is much of that about him in his father's home. Rather, Abraham goes forth under the impetus of the Real. Desire leads Abraham to see an object as desirable, but it is not the object that he desires.

/affetuoso/ What I seek in reality is the Real. That Real, the only true Ethics, is the source of my being, and to follow it is the attempt to be true to one's being. Go, get you forth to a land I will show you.

Home is what I must leave in order to go anywhere but never to arrive. Home is from where I depart from those whom I know and go to those whom I will leave.

/tenerezza/ Isaac, Abraham's son, also lives his life as a veritable homeless wanderer. Isaac leaves his home having been bound and almost sacrificially slaughtered by his father, Abraham, on Mount Moriah. One story tells that following the traumatic event Isaac does not return home with his father, but, rather, descends on the other side of the mountain from Abraham and travels to the home of his brother, Ishmael, who had been at Sarah's insistence cast out by Abraham into the desert. I suspect the two brothers had a great deal to talk about. It is also told that during the three days journey to Moriah undertaken by Abraham and Isaac, Sarah dies, overwhelmed by the news of her husband's intent. Home is what I must leave in order to go anywhere but never to arrive. Home is from where I depart from those whom I know and go to those whom I will leave.

In Ishmael's home, Isaac remains a guest; eventually, he will have to depart. Upon that leaving, Isaac returns "from the vicinity of Beer-lahai-roi, for [Ishmael] was settled in the region of the Negeb." Upon Isaac's return, he meets and marries Rebekah, a woman who has been chosen for him by his father from amongst Abraham's kin. Falling in love at first sight, it is not, however, to his own home that Isaac carries his wife: "And Isaac brought her into the tent of Sarah his mother; he married Rebecca, she became his wife, and he loved her; and thus was Isaac consoled after his mother." Clearly, Rebekah fills not his mother's physical place but the emotional space left by her death. Rebekah becomes the object of Isaac's desire, but he never quite realizes his Desire. He travels nowhere, returning to his mother's tent and his father's home rather than to his own. It is only after Abraham's death that "God blessed Isaac, his son," who then left his father's home and traveled back to Beer-lahai-roi and settled near his brother, Ishmael. Though Isaac does not seem to ever leave home, he also never appears to be at home. Rather than following his own Desire, Isaac seems to be subject to the Desire of others. He re-digs his father's wells. He lives, perhaps, in nostalgia.

Famine plagues the land, however, and Isaac must go in search of sustenance; God commands Isaac not to journey to Egypt where perhaps the food is plentiful, but to remain in Gerar, where he is a stranger, albeit a wealthy one. Should he obey God's command, God promises, "I will be with you and bless you; I will assign all these lands to you and to your heirs, fulfilling the oath that I swore to your father Abraham." For Isaac as for his father Abraham before him, attaining home is a fulfillment in the future. Isaac does not, however, ever acquire the land, and though like his father Isaac becomes quite rich, his success resides in his exile. Isaac lives a nomadic life, living his father's life and not his own, following his father's Desire and not his own. Even as Abraham called Sarah his sister to protect his own life, so does Isaac pass off Rebekah to Abimelech as his sister to protect *his* own life. Isaac might be characterized as the son who returns and repairs the damaged work of the father, but I understand Isaac as the son whose traumatization inhibits his movement out into the world and keeps him tied to the past. It was not Isaac but his father, Abraham, who went forth and never returned. Home is what I must leave in order to go anywhere but never to arrive. Home is from where I depart from those whom I know and go to those whom I will leave. Finally, after only four scriptural chapters, Isaac is gathered to his people after having engendered Jacob and Esau. Like his father before him, Isaac remained homeless, but unlike Abraham, Isaac follows only the Desire of others. He goes nowhere, and is finally buried in Machpelach, the familial sepulchral cave, the only residence in which Isaac has permanence.

/animato/ Finally, the last patriarch, Jacob, confronting the Real, ends up a wanderer for much of his life, always in pursuit and forever acting on Desire. Like his grandfather Abraham, Jacob acquires a new name during his travails—Israel—to mark the self who pursues the Real. Jacob traditionally has been characterized as a deceiver. He obtained Esau's birthright by trading a bowl of red lentil stew to his starving brother, and then, Jacob tricked his aging and blind father, Isaac, into giving him the blessing due the elder brother, Esau. What led Jacob to act in this way could be defined only by Desire;

his duplicity and cruelty should otherwise only be subject to harsh censure. Ironically, the Rabbis will later condemn Esau's duplicity as a way to justify Jacob's actions. Torah itself offers rationale neither for Jacob's callousness to his brother in demanding the birthright in exchange for food, nor for his willing complicity with his mother's deceit to obtain for Jacob the blessing meant for Esau. And Torah does not record any regret on Jacob's part for his actions, but rather, notes only his fear of the consequences. Neither does Torah condemn Jacob for his acts. Indeed, the only semblance of sympathy for the bereft Esau occurs when Torah records, "And Esau said to his father, 'Have you but one blessing, Father? Bless me too, Father!' And Esau wept aloud." Interestingly, Esau will weep later at his reunion with Jacob, but there will be again no record of Jacob's tears. Though Esau's pain is real, he is not offered opportunity for redress nor made the object of any sympathy. Indeed, Esau becomes the archetypical anti-Semite, and Jacob's actions are justified only in retrospect and result. Truth to Desire legitimates callous deception and even, perhaps, cruelty. Jacob is not without serious flaw.

Jacob's life is characterized by trickery, either that selfishly carried out by himself or that which is ultimately practiced upon him. His uncle, Laban, tricks Jacob into marrying his elder daughter, Leah, before Jacob is allowed to marry the younger daughter, Rachel, whom it is said Jacob truly loved (though there are alternative stories about what might have actually happened). Jacob had worked for Laban for seven years and must then agree to work an additional seven years to earn Rachel as his wife. Jacob's effort makes Laban a rich man, but as Jacob complains to Rachel and Leah, "I have served your father with all my might; [though] your father has cheated me, changing my wages time and again." I do not know why Jacob tolerated Laban's deceptions except that perhaps Jacob accepted where his Desire had led him and just awaited it to lead him out to home again.

And then, just as his grandfather before him. Jacob suddenly hears the word of God tell him to "return to the land of your fathers where you were born, and I will be with you." It interests me that now Jacob places full faith in that voice; earlier he had arisen from a dream and said, "God was in this place, and I did not know it." Then, he remained skeptical. After that earlier dream, Jacob actually negotiated with God: "If God remains with me, if God protects me on this journey that I am making, and gives me bread to eat and clothing to wear, and if I return safe to my father's house—the Lord shall be my God." Jacob then had demanded evidence. Perhaps I might say now that in his journeys Jacob had come to trust Desire. When he departs finally from Laban, Jacob employs every means at his disposal: "Jacob kept Laban the Aramean in the dark, not telling him that he was fleeing, and fled with all that he had." Home is what I must leave in order to go anywhere but never to arrive. Home is from where I depart from those whom I know and go to those whom I will leave. Jacob pursues Desire.

≠

/giocoso/ I am myself (but then, who else would I be?) heading out for an adventure in time and space for the weekend. I'm flying to the East Coast to participate in a mini-version of a high school reunion with the . . . well, there rests my dilemma. Do I refer to these eight sixty year old individuals as 'boys,' which is how I last knew them, or should they be called 'men' as they are now. As Dylan says, "Every step of the way we walk the line/Your days are numbered, so are mine." We have many years to say to each other, and for three days will have nowhere to escape. I have no visual image of any of these masculine gendered people (for lack of better words) except those from our adolescent days that expired more than four decades ago. Then, we sat in classes, went to school events, talked about girls and sex, a bit of politics, SAT scores, class rankings and college acceptances. I suspect that after forty years not much has altered. We will still talk about school events, girls and sex, and, perhaps, a bit more about politics. Instead of classes, we will discuss our work, and perhaps we won't compare salaries and awards. I hope we can share what we've learned and would gladly teach. We can talk about the same people, but alas, these, too, we haven't seen in forty years. I suppose we will learn that some have died.

And yet, there have been moments over the past few weeks, when I have thought about this weekend, and there arose in me an emotional wave that borders on tears. When I thought of greeting these men who I haven't seen since they were eighteen year old boys, I imagined a mutuality of embrace which held in its grip the years: we have succeeded all in our way, and have come here to be who we are with those with whom we were. In my thoughts, I wrap my arms about them in greeting, in triumph, and in hope. Our cups runneth over.

Reunions are interesting. They are briefly about the past, a measurement of confirmation. In the moment of meeting again, I assume that this is the person I remember, and I assert that I am the person remembered. We share comrades, events, and some common experiences. We smile knowingly, and sigh over our memories, though I am not certain what meaning is expressed in either smile or sigh.

Quickly, however, the reunion becomes an event about the present, and as we sit around the dinner table with full wine glasses before us, we wonder what it is about us that desires to be friends again. We wonder what our relationship might become now, and we search eagerly for points of interest, for connections, for some emotional linkings. I search longingly into the faces for what I might remember, looking for the person I knew forty years ago, and project the person I am now, although I am still the person from forty years ago. A curious tension, not at all unpleasant.

/animato/ Following Desire, Jacob seems always to be endangered. Esau would have killed him for his deceptions. Jacob had left home under this threat of death and travelled always alone. He dreamt strange dreams! When Jacob finally departs with his large family and flock from his uncle's home, Laban chases after him in fury and accuses him of absconding too stealthily and also of stealing his private gods. Laban threatens Jacob with death. But Jacob, following Desire, cannot be turned back; he will discover home. Rebekah hides the idols *she* has stolen from her father's home so that Jacob can negotiate with Laban.

First, however, Jacob must confront one whom Desire led him to deceive, his brother, Esau. A meeting is set across the Jabbok River. But before the meeting, Jacob dreams again. In an earlier dream, Jacob saw a ladder with angels ascending and descending the rungs. This time, he must actively wrestle with the stranger. He cannot continue home without this engagement. In the fight, Jacob becomes permanently disabled, and in the end, acquires a new name. Home is what I must leave in order to go anywhere but never to arrive. Home is from where I depart from those whom I know and go to those whom I will leave. Following his tussle with the angel, Jacob may now go forward to meet his brother, Esau.

/giocoso/ I have said that I could see the boy in each man here at this reunion, but I realize now that I could also see the man who

evolved from the boy. Of course, there are changes, but we are all palimpsests and, depending on the angle of the light, our layers are more and less visible. I appreciate the complexity that this means for character. As for myself, sometimes in my responses to these men, I move through time and stand as a teen-ager and experience now how I felt then, though now at least I can ascribe to the emotion greater precision and meaning. Then, I experienced a great deal in confusion and muteness. And I sometimes wonder to what extent the others feel this way as well at this meeting. I wished they would be more forthcoming. I refer here to the concept I have labeled as 'leaking,' the willingness to allow our neuroses to be on display rather than to expend energy to hold them in. I am myself (still) concealing. Paradoxically, if I were less neurotic, I would myself be more apt to display my neuroses rather than use my energy to hold them in. Alas, I am not yet so free.

Perhaps these annual meetings serve some defining purpose for us all. We act as a GPS system for each other: we send our signals out and we are located. A voice outside us helps us locate where we are—if only we can understand the accent and we take no offense at the impersonal, mechanical nature of the voice.

After dinner of our last evening together, I sent out my voice. Whether I was found or not remains uncertain—there was a great deal of silence. But, perhaps, then and there, I found the others. I am interested, of course, in how differently we each read our development and understand our own subjectivities, but the only way to ensure an intricate reading is to have written a complex text and to live a full and readable life. There have been moments when I did not have a sense that *I* could be seen as anything but the boy who lived a bit on the margins for what were perceived (by whom, I wonder? Only me?) as inadequacies and failures to arrive. It was my own reading then, even though then the texts were more complex than I could have imagined, and today, now that I understand this palimpsestic reality better, I can read myself and others with greater insight. It improves my satisfaction at meetings.

Each of these boys about this table entered the world he had early designated for his public and private life, and each man achieved a measure of success. Perhaps one thing we learn at these meetings is how to read our achievements with greater degrees of skill and sympathy so that we may continue to acknowledge the lives that are lived and that are brought to our gatherings. If these meetings continue, I hope that we continue to learn how to acknowledge presence, to recognize our entrances and departures, to focus our attention on the conversation of the other, and to recognize his presence. I hope we remain curious, and ask many questions and seriously engage in the responses.

≠

/energico/ With an enormously generous gift—perhaps a bribe—Jacob meets Esau. When Esau sees his brother, he falls on his shoulders and weeps. Everything has reversed. The deceitful kiss Jacob gave his father has become Esau's earnest kiss of reconciliation. Esau's earlier heartbreaking lament and murderous threat is transformed into a heartwarming reunion. Jacob's turbulent Desire has brought him to some Peace. In this reconciliation, Esau urges Jacob to "journey with him home," to set up again a version of the home from which Jacob fled so many years before. But Jacob chooses another direction. He "journeyed on to Succoth, and built a house for himself and made stalls for his cattle; that is why the place is called Succoth." Jacob's Desire compels him to go to the land where his father wandered. When he arrives finally in Shechem, in the land of Canaan, Jacob buys some land and sets up an altar. True to his Desire, Jacob acknowledges that Truth.

When Jacob returns to the place from where his father, Isaac himself, had wandered, Jacob was already 108 years old. Very soon however, the anguish of Joseph's kidnapping turned that very home into a place of torment. "All his sons and daughters sought to comfort him; but he refused to be comforted, saying, "No, I will go down mourning to my son in Sheol." And then, in his final years, Jacob must travel again to Egypt where the long-missing Joseph has become powerful. But Jacob is again a stranger in a strange land. Only upon his death is Jacob permitted to finally rest in the Cave of Machpelach purchased by his grandfather, Abraham. Home is what I must leave in order to go anywhere but never to arrive. Home is from where I depart from those whom I know and go to those whom I will leave. As Rashi says, "Are the righteous not satisfied with what awaits them in the World to Come that they expect to live at ease in this World Too?" Desire in this world always remains unfulfilled; in this life, we seek transcendence of the world by engaging in it.

Perhaps these stories of the patriarchs and matriarchs suggest that home-leaving, the following of Desire, is the moment of transcendence, of acknowledging that we are more than the sum of our past and that we come into being not in our arrival but in our seeking.

My dreams about going home are not at all about returning home, but about keeping myself from home, about being out in the world where I am a stranger and where the work is hard. God and Desire and Transcendence keep me from my place at home. I become agitated and frightened. Where else could I be?

/*mesto*/ Interesting to me, then, is the story of the prodigal son. This well-known parable offers an alternative to Torah's way of thinking about home-leavings and homecomings. There, in the New Testament story, the younger son says to his father, "Let me have the share of the estate that will come to me." The son is motivated to leave by no voice and heads out from home not to achieve greatness but to indulge in profligacy. His desire is base and all too real. There is mention of neither blessing nor purpose in this leaving. I recall that when Abraham left home, it was with all the wealth that *he* had amassed, even with all the souls who would follow *his* Desire. The prodigal son demands not that for which he has worked, but insists on receiving his share of the inheritance, and, having received his portion, he departs, alone. He has nothing to teach; indeed, he has no disciples. It has been said that this request for his inheritance is actually a wish for his father to die. The Catholic priest Henri Nouwen writes, "The son's leaving is . . . a heartless rejection of the home in which the son was born and nurtured and a break with the most precious tradition upheld by the larger community of which he was a part." What distinguishes this home leaving from those of Abraham and Jacob is that the prodigal son takes nothing of *his own*, while Abraham and Jacob take nothing that is *not* their own. If Abram breaks with the tradition of his father and the larger community of which he was a part, he does not necessarily break with his father and wish him dead. Abram leaves home to become Abraham and Jacob to become Israel. But the prodigal son hears no voice; he simply rejects all he has ever known and believed. He converts no one, and when he finally arrives at the place to which he is drawn, he does not labor, but rather loses all that he possessed in debauchery and self-serving pleasure.

Perhaps this profligacy was available only away from home, but then I would say that what this son sought in leaving home involved not a transcendence at all, but rather, just some distance and a little ready cash. The prodigal son sinks into what is easily available to satisfy his too, too, solid flesh, with what he realizes finally, is ephemeral and disappointingly unsatisfying; when his monetary supply runs out, he has no resources on which to draw. Driven not by Desire, but from a refusal to experience Desire, wishing to bury Desire beneath the sensual things of this world, this son is not rootless; rather, this son is merely profligate. There is in his actions no notion of transcendence, though in his debauchery, there might be a yearning for oblivion. Home is what I must leave in order to go anywhere but never to arrive. Home is from where I depart from those whom I know and go to those whom I will leave. This prodigal son does not so much leave home as escape it, though what he runs from does not lead him towards that to which he runs.

Eventually having wasted his inheritance and fallen into wretched poverty, the prodigal son seeks employment in order to survive, but he cannot earn the means for subsistence. Having indulged himself in satisfying his sensuous pleasures, the prodigal son can think of nothing beyond his condition in the immediate present. Unlike Jacob, this prodigal son tolerates no difficulty and little frustration. I recall that Jacob, too, left home under dubious circumstances, but he became a highly skilled shepherd, transformed his kinsman and employer, Laban, into a very rich man. And to acquire what he sought, Jacob tolerated hard work, deception as cruel as he had practiced, deprivation and frustration. Jacob's arduous labor served him well, and when he finally departed from Laban's home, Jacob left with a large family for whom he was responsible, as well as with a very respectable herd of sheep and of goats. I wonder what skills the prodigal son possessed to offer for employment; what had he done in his short life? What does he seem prepared to learn to earn his bread? Actually, he becomes unemployed; perhaps he is unemployable.

Alone and far from home, destitute and helpless, this prodigal son finally "came to his senses" and to himself said, "How many of my father's hired men have the food they want and more, and here am I dying of hunger! I will leave this place and go to my father and say: Father I have sinned against heaven and against you; I no longer deserve to be called your son; treat me as one of your hired men." It interests me that the story announces that the prodigal son, now starving and desperate, *came to his senses*, as if his leaving home originally was the result of his having taken *leave* of his senses...as if in his present condition the only rational and reasonable thing to do is to go back home...as if in his present circumstances, there is no sound alternative but to return home. This prodigal son can imagine nothing but to go home to be cared for by his father, and is suddenly incensed that even the servants, who for many years labored in his father's household, were better cared for and well fed that he. And how certain this son seems to be that he will find acceptance and employment at his father's house; how certain he seems that he will be welcome and, even more importantly, fed and cared for there, even as his father feeds and cares for the hired men! This return stems not from following Desire but from more pursuit of the immediate and the mundane. Indeed, the prodigal son's refusal of Desire all along has precluded his ever achieving much of anything.

Now, the return of the prodigal son inspires a great celebration, and ironically, the father throws an elaborate and sensuous feast to celebrate the homecoming. Seeing his son afar off (I wonder how the father knew to look for his wayward son, or was he just looking out on the horizon and recognized him?), he "ran to his boy, clasped him in his arms and kissed him." And although the prodigal son cries that he "has sinned against heaven and against you," the father said to his servants "Quick! Bring out the best robe and put it on him; put a ring on his finger and sandals on his feet. Bring the calf we have been fattening, and kill it; we will celebrate by having a feast, because this son of mine was dead and has come back to life; he was lost and is found." This celebration appears not unlike the life in which the prodigal son has engaged and that has led to his ruin and from which he has recently departed. This son who has overindulged in immediate and sensual pleasures is immersed again in the sensual. I wonder for whom the calf had been originally fattened, and what celebration the father had planned? Certainly, there is nothing in this family's history that suggests that revelry and festival had been customary practice.

And when the older son returns home from his day of labor, he hears from afar the loud celebratory proceedings. When he inquires of the servant the cause of the party only to discover it marks the return of his younger brother, the older son is enraged and refuses to enter the house and join the festivities. He says to his father, "I have slaved for you and never once disobeyed any order of yours, yet you never offered me so much as a kid for me to celebrate with my friends. But this son of yours, when he comes back after swallowing up your property—he and his loose women—you kill the calf we had been fattening." And the father responds not consolingly, "Your brother here was dead and has come to life; he was lost and is found." Far from home, the prodigal son was lost, but when returned home, he is again found. Home is what I must leave in order to go anywhere but never to arrive. Home is from where I depart from those whom I know and go to those whom I will leave. At home, of course, the prodigal son learned only to stay home, witness the fate of his older brother, and even when the prodigal son moved away from it, he did not get very far. Now returned home, I wonder what will he now do?

Of course, despite the father's invitation, the older son remains unsatisfied, but then, he too has seemingly never acted on his Desire. By his own admission, he has obeyed all of his father's orders; he has done nothing of his own. I suspect he has spent much of his life in frustration and unhappiness, and lived thwarted and dissatisfied, suppressing Desire. Indeed, the older son has spent his life pursuing the Desire of his Father, and has never left home. Perhaps, even, he has ceased to dream. Home is what I must leave in order to go anywhere but never to arrive. Home is from where I depart from those whom I know and go to those whom I will leave.

I was once an elder son.

/animato/ Jacob is a younger son, as are so many sons in ascendancy in Torah. Jacob belongs to the founding patriarchy of Judaism. The God in whom Jews believe is the God repeatedly referred to as the God of Abraham, Isaac and Jacob. It is in very odd ways that these men (and their matriarchal wives), however, serve as role models. To me, it has been long clear that neither these revered men nor their wives are portrayed without careful and thorough depiction of their considerable and sometimes serious human flaws. If the character of the Greek pantheon of gods suffers from human peccadilloes, then the Jewish patriarchy and matriarchy has these same failings in their very human form. This is often a relief to me. I have always felt it better to have real people as heroes with human failings I can recognize than to maintain images of perfection who have nothing to do with me or my mortal associates. However, Scriptural reference does raise some serious questions about their example. And the homes from which each derives and which each creates leave much to be desired.

I am reviewing the situation. I have a few questions.

Of all the patriarchs, Jacob is to me the most vexatious and his home-leavings and homecomings so problematic. He is a deceiver and a trickster, a brazen and cold-hearted opportunist. Jacob cheats Esau, his older brother, out of both his birthright and his father's blessing. The former he gains by selling Esau food when he appeared to be starving. Of the ethics of this act I am doubtful. I am reminded of Woody Allen's proud display of his pocket watch. "See this," he says, pulling out of his pants pocket a gold watch attached to a gold chain. After a slight pause, he adds, "My grandfather *sold me* this watch on his deathbed!" Esau acknowledges that were he dead his birthright would serve no purpose, and so he must have expected that Jacob would have let him die of starvation unless he assigned to Jacob the birthright due the eldest son. The narrative doesn't offer any insight into Esau's response to the transaction, nor does it suggest that Esau attempted to renege on the bargain. Indeed, Esau seems to deal honestly with his cruel and deceitful brother, Jacob.

And then Jacob conspires to steal their father Isaac's blessing from Esau by staging an elaborate, even heinous charade. Isaac, knowing he will soon die, requests his elder son, Esau, to prepare him the meal he loves so well, to feed him this repast, and to receive his blessing. Overhearing her husband's conversation with Esau, Rachel urges Jacob to follow her lead and to feed his father a dish that *she* will prepare. Jacob then dresses in his brother's clothes, so that he might smell like Esau, and Rachel adorns Jacob with the skin of an animal to replicate Esau's rough and hairy complexion. "I am Esau, your first born. Pray sit up and eat of my game, that you may give me your innermost blessing," Jacob says to his father deceivingly. And Isaac eats and blesses Jacob with Esau's blessing. When his first-born son arrives with the dish *he* has prepared, Isaac has already eaten and given to Jacob the blessing promised Esau. It interests me that when the now confused Isaac asks of Esau "Who are you," he answers, "I am your son, Esau, your first born." Esau acknowledges first his filial position. But Jacob, in his response to his father's query, had omitted this relationship, perhaps unwilling to assume this aspect of the charade, or subtly denying his patrimony.

Esau becomes justifiably enraged and threatens to kill his brother. There is in Torah precedent for the violence provoked by sibling rivalries. But perhaps this story of siblings suggests that murder is not a means to any end, and hence, *Genesis* offers an alternative narrative. Jacob's mother and co-conspirator, Rebekah, urges Jacob to leave lest he suffer harm, and Jacob leaves home with a brief farewell to his aged father though he does not kiss him. I can only imagine the haste and stealth with which the preparations for escape are made, and the quick farewell Jacob offered his mother, Rebekah, who had perhaps traveled to where Jacob was hiding from his brother's murderous wrath. I suspect Jacob kissed his mother good-bye and departed in the still of a moonless and starless night. He will not see her alive again. And he will not see his father again until he stands with his brother Esau at Isaac's grave at Machpelah. Home is what I must leave in order to go anywhere but never to arrive. Home is from where I depart from those whom I know and go to those whom I will leave.

I wonder why Rebekah does not fear Esau. After all, she was a co-conspirator and equally culpable for the wrong done to her older son. She cannot depend on Isaac's protection; he is clearly powerless. She must have confidence that Esau will do her no violence. Nor does Esau accuse his father of some stupidity and ignorance for having been dupe to such wiles. How could you not know the difference between Jacob and myself, you foolish old man? But I wonder what kind of home it must have been for Esau with a powerless father, an apparently distant mother, and a sibling rivalry characterized by open hostility. This must have been an easy home from which to depart. I wonder whether Torah does not suggest in this story and the several that come before it that families are problematic and contentious and that only in leaving does one gain opportunity. Disillusioned, Esau, too, leaves home.

/malinconico/ What is striking about the opening line of the chorus of John Denver's song is its directness. "I'm leaving on a jet plane." In an interesting way, the rest of the chorus is superfluous. Leaving as opposed to going, leaving as opposed to traveling. Not on an airplane, which would suggest domesticity, but on a jet plane that involves speed and irretrievable distance. I do not think there is in these lines any hope of return.

Indeed, the second line completes the first: "Don't know if I'll be back again." This is a permanent rupture, even an abrupt departure, not with acrimony nor from argument, but out of some inner necessity that defines the one who leaves.

But the plaintiveness of the sentiment, "Oh, babe, I hate to go," tears at my heart. (To me, the heart is where these things do hurt. While I might be interested scientifically why this might be, I am certain nonetheless that phenomenologically this is where I will locate the pain's location.) With regret, but inevitably, the leaving must occur. "I hate to wake you up to say goodbye," and so there is finally, no goodbye, just the leaving.

I always find leaving home difficult—so many things tie us to the place, though I entertain with delight the *anticipation* of leaving. Perhaps it is that I consider traveling a sort of disappearance, and the more miles I place between me and home, the more disappeared I feel. Away from home perhaps, I am not the person I am at home, and in the traveling, I move to whom I am not yet. When someone else in my family travels, I am often oppressed by my sameness.

|lacrimoso| After almost forty years of separation, Esau and Jacob are to meet again across the River Jabbok. Why is Jacob here in this place at all? Isn't the desert vast enough to avoid having to cross paths with Esau? If Jacob had such great fear, why not avoid the confrontation altogether and circumvent the meeting? What in Jacob demands this feared, yet seemingly necessary, reunion? It is not nostalgia that impels Jacob to this meeting. Jacob prepares for it by expecting the worse: he divides up his retinue and sends them on along, remaining himself alone on the far side of the river. Is this cowardice or strategy, I wonder? Jacob wrestles with the angel, whom many interpreters hold is the spirit of Esau, and having at least not *lost* the battle, he demands from the stranger a blessing; he receives instead a new name, Israel. It is this name that will become that of the nation. The next day, Jacob crosses the Jabbok, and we read, "Esau ran to greet him. He embraced him and falling on his neck, he kissed him; and they wept." Why is the action described from the perspective of Esau, I wonder. Other than Jacob's having wept, (perhaps less out of affection than out of relief that his brother, whom he had viciously tricked out of his birthright and his blessing, did not kill him), there is no record of Jacob's emotional response to the reunion? Why doesn't the Torah record anything but Jacob's fear of Esau's retribution? There is a curious perspectival shift in the story here from that of Jacob to that of Esau. The Torah seems conflicted concerning this reunion. I have myself a few questions.

|giocoso| Another homecoming event: A whirlwind organizing campaign was taking place to stage a reunion for the 1965-66 graduating classes of Goshen High School. I am a member of the former, and due to prior commitments that I wouldn't consider forgoing for a minute, I could not attend.

Every day, names from the distant past would cross my desktop. People I had not thought about in forty years appeared suddenly before me. Sometimes they even talked to me. Of course, I couldn't see any of them except as seventeen year olds, but they kept mentioning their grandchildren and their retirement homes, and there developed a serious divide between my memory and the reality about which I now read. These people began to occupy my dreams and disturbed my days.

The search for graduates indicated that some of my former classmates have kept in touch over the years. Someone seemed to know where someone else was presently living. They seemed to know about those who were no longer living. When I gazed back over this huge expanse of time and across the chasm, I saw nothing except the other side of forty-one years. There was nothing moving between those two points, no companions, no landmarks, and no sounds. And this awareness caused me discomfort. I was disoriented as forty years imposed itself on me unawares and unbidden. There are emotions I experience now that I must have vigorously repressed, and there was something about the conversation on line that reproduced some of my adolescent angst and insecurities and terrors. Suddenly, I was thrust back there, even though I thought that I had moved on, dammit. What would I do at a reunion with people I had not seen in forty one years? Why hadn't I seen them in forty-one years? Ah, there's the rub, isn't it?

/mesto/ I remember, as if it were yesterday, screening the movie *Same Time, Next Year*. This 1978 film by Robert Mulligan, starring Alan Alda and Ellen Burstyn, portrayed the annual, romantic tryst of a man and a woman, each married to a different person, who sometime in the 1950s happen to discover themselves in bed engaged in sexual activity, and who then continue to meet in the same room on the same date every year for the next twenty-five or so years. For one weekend every year—same time, next year, they intone to each other upon departing—these two reunite to . . . well, that is the issue for me right now. Why do they maintain this relationship? Are they coming home or leaving it? Do they know the difference? I never got the sense that it was the fantastic sex that brought them to these homecomings, though even in 1978 such a suggestion was not something polite society acknowledged, at least the society to which I belonged. The two characters do not seem to share an intellectual life, nor do I think they read the same books—well, if they read books at all. During these rendezvous, they do exchange personal headlines reporting the significant occurrences that have taken place to each of them in the past year, and these communications inspire the appropriate response from the other while offering some shallow catharsis for the audience. These were perplexing, traumatic times in the United States, and so over the twenty-five years of their relationship, we observe the steadily (even rapidly) changing social mores and beliefs which made up and sundered society's fabric. In fact, the characters in the film are mere emblems, a means to display the social changes rather than actually explore them, and the film manipulates the audience into a shallow, nostalgic, solipsistic miasma that obscures the complexities of the social, political and psychological order in a superficial image of conflict and change exemplified in the relationship of this politically correct couple. Ah, yes, the audience sighs comfortably, I remember: that is exactly how it was. The film exploits nostalgia.

It was a terrible movie, sentimental, and false as all nostalgic movies must be. These productions do not portray reality, but only the perception of how reality might have been if only there were no real conflict or context. But I don't mean to talk about the film. I want to address here the film's premise: same time, next year.

I suppose that somewhere out there out there exist individuals who can sustain such a relationship, but I cannot understand how it might be accomplished. I cannot comprehend how it could be possible to live separately and without any contact for an entire year, one filled with an immensity of details and incredible (even incomprehensible and unspeakable) complexities, and then to come together for a single weekend into an intimate situation and behave as if the whole previous year of absence and silence had not occurred at all. "Now, where were we before we were so rudely interrupted by our lives?" I have always thought that intimacy results from behavior as well as intention, and that true intimacy—the kind intimated in the film as occurring during the yearly trysts—requires consistent effort and regular vulnerability and an engagement and sharing of daily living in what is for most an ordinary life. Otherwise, I think, such occasional occasions become the business of catch-up. There is no development. In the film, the relationship is static because it lacks real life. They may serve the fatted calf, but they are not home, and when they leave wherever they are staying it is as if they had not been there.

The issue: how to expect the intimacy of a relationship to be sustained *and even to grow* when there is no contact and sharing and leaking enjoyed during the very long periods of time *between* meetings. Is it true that there could be no other place or time to have any contact whatsoever? What is the function of such yearly meetings if there has been no development of any intimacy in the time prior to the meeting? Couldn't I find such conversation closer to home? Here, the film's actions serve merely to portray the changing times, though the people never do really change at all. What is finally gained by such annual assignations except the marking of Time? For Thoreau, since the pursuit of perfection made time irrelevant, these meetings could have nothing to do with perfection.

≈

/energico/ This meeting of Jacob and Esau at the Jabbok continues to intrigue me. It is a homecoming about which I have a few questions. Jacob sends his messengers to Esau with directions to inform the older brother of Jacob's recent history. "I have stayed with Laban for the past twenty years and remained until now; I have acquired cattle, asses, sheep, and male and female slaves; and I send this message to my lord in the hope of gaining your favor." Is it possible that Esau did not know any of this chronicle? I doubt it. Their father, Isaac, knew where to find his brother, Ishmael, when Isaac fled Abraham following the binding! Indeed, Esau seems somehow aware of Jacob's presence: when the messengers return to Jacob they inform him that Esau is at that moment coming to meet *him*! And it is *not* a foreign force Esau is preparing to meet; he knows it is his brother Jacob. And I suspect also that Esau knows enough about his Uncle Laban to know that his uncle is a man not to be trusted. I like to think that in his message Jacob is subtly suggesting that he suffered trickery as had Esau. Esau must have known some details concerning Jacob's history and even his present movements. Interestingly, Jacob seems to have remained unaware of the life of Esau. If there was talk about family around Laban's tables, then Torah gives no hint of it. Jacob had, indeed, left home wholly behind. So, perhaps this present meeting acknowledges that complete repudiation is not possible; Jacob must effect some reconciliation with his familial past before he can move on. Indeed, the wrestle with the stranger might be interpreted as Jacob's struggle with his own conscience. In this first communication with Esau, Jacob might be indicating that he has learned something and that reunion is possible.

Jacob showed great fear at the news of his brother's imminent arrival, accompanied as Esau was by 400 men. The Rabbis tell us that Jacob feared that he and his family would be harmed or that he might be forced to harm Esau in self-defense. The latter possibility seems to ignore Jacob's wrestle with the stranger the previous evening, and the former thought indicates Jacob's acknowledgment of the wrong he had committed years ago. And wouldn't Jacob's attempt to purchase Esau's favor suggest that Jacob had learned nothing? Jacob's message contains no trace of familiarity or contrition, and admits to no acknowledgment of a shared history. Rather, the message seems to consist of some telegraphic news of Jacob's arrival with his considerable retinue. The message contains news but no concern. After almost twenty years, why is *this* the content of the first communication between these brothers who parted so hastily and in circumstances so charged with animosity and fear? Jacob assumes some knowledge of his brother in his belief that his gift will appeal to his brother and effect some ease of passage for Jacob, but there is nothing of reconciliation in Jacob's communication. This is no homecoming.

For the past twenty years, Jacob has been living with his mother's brother, Laban, to whom he escaped following the cruel ruse he perpetrated on Esau, his brother. Once arrived and seated at Laban's hearth, Jacob told Laban his story. It appears that this is the only time Jacob mentions family. But Laban's response to the story is curious to me. He says, "You are truly my flesh and bone." I can only assume that the trickery and deception that Jacob and his mother practiced on Esau and Isaac is familiar to Laban, and in his comment, he might be acknowledging Jacob's kinship with him. Were Jacob a wiser man, he might have then known to be wary of Laban.

Laban quickly brings Jacob into his household—does Jacob consider this invitation a homecoming?—and Jacob begins to work for his uncle. Within a month, Laban offers Jacob recompense for his work, and Jacob asks for the hand in marriage of Laban's younger daughter, Rachel, with whom Jacob has fallen in love. Laban quickly accedes, and Jacob offers to work seven years for Laban in exchange. "Better that you work for me who is family than you work for someone else," says Jacob's uncle, and the deal seems to be made. But for Jacob, engagement in this family turns out to be a trap: on Jacob's wedding day, Laban deceives him, even as Jacob had deceived his father, and at the wedding ceremony Laban substitutes the veiled older daughter, Leah for Rachel, as Jacob had once disguised himself as Esau. Jacob marries the wrong woman even as Isaac had blessed the wrong son. Why in Jacob's first message to his brother does he tell Esau that he has been staying at their Uncle's house? Is he offering sympathy or demanding it?

I've got a few questions. Why does Jacob move his entire retinue through territory clearly controlled by Esau? Jacob must have known he was entering territory in proximity to his brother, Esau. He must have known something of his brother to send this type of message. In this first communication between the brothers in twenty years, Jacob refers to his brother as "My lord, Esau." Is Jacob being *too* deferential? Is his humility *too* false? Is Jacob again practicing some dissimulation? But then, he had been with Laban for twenty years and must have learned a great deal about deception and dissimilitude.

I've also been wondering about Esau's life after Jacob left home. The Torah portion, *Tol'dot*, tells us that Esau, too, left his family and went to Ishmael (the tribe not the man), there to take a wife, knowing that this act would displease his father. Esau lived there, very far from home. In sending Esau to live amongst this tribe, Torah draws a connection between Ishmael, the banished son, and Esau, the abandoned one. What is the connection between banishment and abandonment? Perhaps they are merely different sides of leaving home?

When the brothers meet, Esau asks to be introduced to the groups of people traveling with Jacob and then wonders what Jacob means by greeting his brother with such a huge retinue. I think Esau seems to long for some reconciliation and to resume some familial affection. But Jacob avoids this possibility, saying that all that he travels with is merely his gift to his brother, "To gain my lord's favor." Esau refuses the offer, saying that he already has all that he needs, and Esau humbly begs Jacob to keep what he has for himself. Jacob, however, insists, and Esau finally accepts the gift.

I know that it is very hard to accept a gift sometimes—often at times more difficult to accept than to give. To receive a gift is often assumed to mean accepting obligation; we feel as if we have been encumbered in accepting the gift. I know why Jacob, given his character and recent history, might believe this. But I think Esau sincerely has no interest in Jacob's offer; Esau is content to be reunited with his brother. And Jacob's insistence that Esau accept his gift smacks to me of an insincere offer. The 'gift' is in fact a 'bribe.' Esau's emotional response to seeing Jacob is not reciprocated. Jacob vies again for advantage, continues to prevaricate, manipulate, and respond with disingenuousness. He shows no desire to reconcile; he only wants safe passage. Home is what I must leave in order to go anywhere . . . . My heart breaks for Esau, the older brother. I am an older brother.

Esau invites Jacob to his home with all his family and flocks and servants. "Let us start on our journey, and I will proceed at your pace." Esau understands that Jacob is traveling with his children.

He shows concern, even some understanding. Jacob suggests that his pace will be too slow; if Esau will travel ahead at a faster pace, Jacob will soon follow. Jacob is not telling the truth. Esau begs Jacob to allow him to leave some of his own people behind to assist Jacob on his way, but again, Jacob refuses the offer. Jacob continues to deceive.

The plan had been to meet at Esau's home in Seir, but Jacob does not travel to his brother's home. "Jacob journeyed on to Succoth, and built a house for himself, and made stalls for his cattle." Esau waited endlessly for his brother to arrive. What must he have felt as he waited for his brother's return? When did he realize he had again been tricked?

Or perhaps Jacob knew that to return to even his brother's home was to enter back into the web of behaviors from which he barely managed to escape twenty years earlier. During the evening prior to this eventful meeting between the estranged brothers, Jacob has struggled with his demons, or his conscience, or even the specter of his brother Esau, and triumphed: he is no longer Jacob but Israel. He is a new man, and that new man must avoid entering into and re-engaging in old patterns. That Jacob's new name, Israel, becomes the name of the nation suggests Torah's acknowledgement that home must be transcended if one is to attempt to create home. Home is what I must leave in order to go anywhere but never to arrive. Home is from where I depart from those whom I know and go to those whom I will leave.

Alas, Jacob will engage as a father in the same /lacrimoso/ egregious behaviors that led to his subterfuge and escape many years earlier. He will show favor to one son and create filial contention and hatred. Brother will be set against brother. And Jacob will be subject to the deceptions of his children and to the anguish of loss even as his own father had experienced these sorrows. And perhaps in these stories Torah suggests there is no escape from family ties or sins, though there is courage and finally some reward in the attempt. I suppose the Rabbis admire Jacob's pursuit of his Desire though they seem quite aware that achieving Desire is impossible.

But I ache for Esau. His attempt at reconciliation with his brother is rebuffed. What Esau had long ago sold, and what he lost through trickery, seems to have been forgotten in his desire for some connection to home. It might be that whatever home he has built remains incomplete without Jacob. Perhaps Esau is trying to establish a relationship that has no precedent in order to fill somehow his own sense of original loss. It is a fruitless attempt, however. Having perpetrated deception and having had deception perpetrated on him, Jacob remains guarded and unwilling to renew affiliation. He would remain outside, and without a home.

/*grazioso*/ To leave home behind, I have thought, makes possible the discovery of home everywhere. My friend, Henry David Thoreau wrote: "If you are ready to leave father and mother, and brother and sister, and wife and child and friends, and never see them again—if you have paid your debts, and made your will, and settled all your affairs, and are a free man, then you are ready for a walk." I recall that Abraham embarked on such a walk. This leave–taking need not necessarily be a physical absence—it *is* simply a walk that Thoreau advocates—but an emotional leave-taking—one must be wholly unencumbered and be prepared to leave *everything* behind. Perhaps this is the walk Jacob undertakes by refusing Esau's hospitality. Perhaps the dream in which I am drawn back home suggests that I am not prepared to engage in that walk. In my dream, I always know where I am. I am Jacob. who earlier in his travels from home, dreamed and awoke to note that "God was in this place and I did not know it." In my dreams, I am not lost in physical space, but lost, perhaps, in psychic or spiritual space, disoriented and disturbingly estranged. In the dream, that place to which I want to return is designated 'home,' though I do not think that it is my home that I seek. Desire was in this place and I did not know it. Or perhaps in the dream the home from which I am separated is the home I have not yet known. And Jacob went on and settled in Succoth. Though I am an older son, perhaps in my dreams I am more Jacob than Esau.

Though home might be traditionally understood as a place of ultimate return ("Home is where when you go there, they have to take you in," the poet Robert Frost writes in "Death of the Hired Hand"), home need not be identified with that return but, rather, can now be valued as a setting forth. If in my dream I seek to return home but cannot achieve a homecoming, then perhaps in my waking life I experience some absence, some lack, that to achieve 'home' will fill, however it is that I define 'home.' My dreams depict my yearning. Without that longing, there would be in life no impetus to move, and that would be equivalent to death. Desire sends me *out* from a settled place of home rather than draws me back to it. I can call that lack Desire, which because it may be only known by what it is not, may be constitutive of my unconsciousness. My desire is always displaced onto an object that desire makes visible, but Desire itself remains unseen and even unknown. However, when I acquire the object, my desire is not satiated or gone. Desire is never known, but always pursued. It is not chocolate which activates my desire, but my desire that defines chocolate as the desired object. My desire in the dream is not for home, but in the dream home is the object of my desire.

Desire may be constituted by the inevitable and irrevocable loss of the attachment to the mother's breast. When there is no absence between the child and the breast, there is no Desire. But when the breast is no longer available, then what remains as a consequence of the separation is Desire, and that Desire seeks an impossible union and unattainable happiness. Desire arises out of that loss and that absence. Desire is constituted by that non-presence, and therefore, its 'reality' can never be articulated. In this sense, Desire may be thought of as a motive and not a thing; in this sense, desire can be linked to transcendence. Desire sends me out from home seeking for something beyond me that will never be realized but for which I continue to search. To pursue desire, then, is to maintain faith. Perhaps in my dream I cannot get home, and so I awaken to continue the dream that I have a home that I seek.

Desire always leads me to move beyond my present self as it has become defined by some past, and in this sense, Desire is a quest for what I do not yet know and must yet learn. I can rationally define my goal, but I can define that goal only in retrospect. We know ourselves always in retrospect, but ironically, when we attain this knowledge, we are no longer there. We have already moved someplace else. We have made ourselves strangers in a strange land. In this perspective, home is that toward which we always head but never arrive until too late; alas, upon arrival, we are no longer there. Home is what I must leave in order to go anywhere but never to arrive. Home is from where I depart from those whom I know and go to those whom I will leave.

In his work in philosophy and theology, Rabbi Abraham Joshua Heschel posits an unknowable self realized in action but understood partly and temporarily only in retrospect. He writes: "All we know of the self is its expression, but the self is never fully expressed. What we are, we cannot say; what we become, we cannot grasp. It is all a cryptic, suggestive abbreviation which the mind tries in vain to decipher." Our goal is to become the self, though this achievement can never be completed. That home to which I cannot return I don't really know. If it is where I head, I know not where I go but only that I go. Home is always beyond me, though the route to it begins in the mundane, diurnal world. Heschel again: "It is not from experience but from *our inability to experience* what is given to our mind that certainty of the realness of God is derived. It is not the order of being but the transcendent in the contingency of all order, the allusions to transcendence in all acts and all things that challenge our deepest understanding." It is always in what *else* is suggested in the things of this world, the surplus, that the hints of my Desire are recognized. Desire is the self that I do not yet know but for which I quest. I do not know who I am, and I continue to seek that knowledge of myself. In the present in my effort to find meaning in existence, I do not understand wholly my life or myself. "The essence of what I am is not mine. *I am what is not* mine. I am that I am not . . ." Heschel teaches me. We are always more than we know, but less than we can ever be. Limitless insatiable Desire is also illimitable, insatiable faith. Home is what I must leave in order to go anywhere but never to arrive. Home is from where I depart from those whom I know and go to those whom I will leave. In this perspective, my dreams are not about return but about its limitless impossibility. I will never get home, thank God.

/grandioso/ My idea of home derives from all and none of the homes that I have experienced; home is the object of my desire but no single home (or even all of them) can contain that desire. I must go forth from my home. There is precedence for such leavings.

SECOND MOVEMENT
Marche Funebre

/mesto/ Who would know the hour of his death?

Even for Wisconsin, this wintry day was cold. Though it was already noon, the thermometer had barely passed zero, and the lack of sun only made more painful the absence of degrees. The day was palpably grey, and its pallor drained the color out of even the billboards whose very purpose was to catch my attention. Though the drive was long, I had not bothered to turn on the radio; I preferred the forced isolation of the car and the pervasive oppression of the shrouded day. As was my wont, always fearful of being late, I arrived too early. Time, my own or some else's, has its urgencies.

But perhaps I have used the possessive incorrectly here. How can time belong to anyone? Thoreau claimed that time was the stream into which he went fishing. Rapidly moving water cannot be possessed by anyone, though it is there in its depths where that for which I seek lives. And whether I throw in my line or not is really of no concern to the river; it will flow regardless. I can act in time, but I cannot hold it. And time is remarkably oblivious of any performance of mine or of others. Lady Macbeth cautions her husband, "To beguile the time, Look like the Time," but it is not time but themselves that they mean to deceive. Time is not complicit in their plans, though it might be pretty to think so. The murderous plot they devise depends first on their capacity to deceive themselves and each other: they fool themselves to think that it is Time they would fool. Time has nothing to do with their efforts; Time is merely present. They and we can only act within it and then assume responsibility—or not—for our actions. It was Cassius who more correctly said, "The fault, dear Brutus, is not in the stars but in ourselves, methinks." Time is and does not.

In their endless study of God's world and the lives it sustains, the Rabbis note that the text does *not* say 'let there be evening and morning,' but rather, "And there was evening and there was morning, the first day," From this, the Rabbis assert that Time existed even before the creation of the first day. In the Rabbis' formulation, Time remains independent of even the universe and we mortals have no effect on it. Had the Macbeths considered this, they might have avoided their tragedy. They depended too much on the innocence of time and hoped that in their actions they could deceive it and avoid all consequences.

/*lamentoso*/ My drive in the Wisconsin cold was to attend the rites of one who had abandoned Time.

/*mesto*/ Piles of snow had reduced the size of the parking lot, and I eased my car into a space somewhere by the middle of the building and mid-way between the synagogue set back from the highway and the service road. I was conscious only of the hearse and the black stretch limousine parked with feigned discretion too conspicuously to my left, over in a corner slightly behind the building and out of familiar view. These dark vehicles incompletely hidden reminded me of toughs waiting in the shadowy alleys to pounce upon unsuspecting passers-by. I assumed that the other parked, black cars had delivered the grieving family and its immediate extensions. I cautiously reached down onto the passenger seat, grabbed my kippah and exchanged it for the hat atop my head. Abandoning the warmth of the car, I stepped out into the frigid air and headed for the door. From the other side of the parking lot, several others who had also arrived too early walked toward the shul doors, and I held the door open as they passed in. I did not recognize any of them, but nodded silently and familiarly just the same. No one offered a smile.

On the right just inside the door, was the coatroom. I hung up my dark winter coat on a thin, wire hanger. Around its shoulders, I placed the winter scarf so that amongst the many other dark winter coats, I might easily find my own garment after the service. I placed my hat in the coat sleeve, and walked toward the sanctuary. The coffin in which the body of my friend Mark Abrahamson now lay sat before the door of the sanctuary room, set against the wall where on Shabbat stood the stand on which the congregation's prayer shawls were hung. The coffin was covered in a white cloth not unlike an expensive bed-sheet, but underneath I knew rested the cloaked plain pine box prescribed for traditional Jewish funerals. Standing in front of the coffin, I don't remember feeling very much at all. No, I thought, he isn't there.

/mesto/ Who would know the hour of his death? Mark knew the time to the minute. He chose the hour and even the means of his demise. He was found hanging from a pipe in the basement of his home. He was fifty-six years old.

His death irrevocably altered my view of the world, and forever destroyed the security in which I had previously stood.

When I received the phone call informing me of his death, I assumed Mark had suffered a heart attack; these days almost every one with whom I keep company lives in this neighborhood. I knew he had physical ailments—mostly issues of breathing and asthma. And I knew he suffered from depression—who doesn't these days—and that he took medication to relieve his condition. I also keep a refillable prescription of anti-anxiety pills at my bedside for those late night/early morning angst-ridden attacks that trouble my rest. I had understood that some motive for the psychotropic medications was associated with Mark's physical conditions, and that his breathing difficulties were considerably relieved by the treatment. I had always thought him sane enough, and so, when the call came on that Wednesday evening saying that Mark had died (and as I continue to live I know that these calls will continue to arrive), I assumed the cause a result of some physical breakdown. I was shocked and saddened by his death. After all, I am myself of a similar age, and his death confronted me with my own mortality; his son is the same age as my daughter. They—we—had been friends.

And then in stunned phone calls, news began to trickle in that his death had not occurred from natural causes, but had been, in fact, a suicide. Mark had lately suffered episodes of severe depression and recently had hospitalized himself in a desperate attempt to manage the condition. It was rumored that he had changed his medications and that he had in the last several weeks ceased going into the office to try to relieve his stress—I considered whether this latter act was symptom or cure. People had been worried at his appearance.

Everything just seemed to have fallen apart and I guess he had neither strength nor desire to put anything back together again. That Wednesday morning, his wife had arrived home after dropping their son off at school and had found Mark hanging from a basement pipe.

I couldn't help but wonder what he had said to his son as he left that day for school. I wondered if he had kissed him and wished him well. Had he said, "See you later?" Had he even said, "Goodbye?" I thought of Dylan's "Restless Farewell:" "But the bottles are done/We killed each one/And the table's full and overflowed./And the corner sign/Says its closing time./So I'll bid farewell and be down the road." In Dylan's farewell, I have always heard finality and hope, but in Mark's leave-taking, though there was finality, there was no fullness or hope. He had left too many unanswerable questions which are substantively different than unanswered ones. The former allowed for no pursuit.

What happened?

I had always believed that Mark enjoyed a comfortable marital life, though I clearly recalled a conversation (or two) over dinners shared by only the two of us in which he voiced his doubts and concerns and even, fears regarding marriage. But what rational person doesn't have such thoughts? What he had now done seemed to me so irrational. Then, I had taken his conversations as the mark of his sanity. And whenever I saw him and Anya together, they enacted an intimacy I envied. I saw no dangerous rents in their fabric. What happened? His suicide suggested to me that he had hated his life, but she was that life, wasn't she? Or at least a good part of it!

I couldn't bring up in my mind the Mark who hanged himself. Whenever I thought of him, I could only envision the bearded, cuddly man shuffling into shul, seemingly at ease, smiling at everyone as he turned his head like a searchlight, looking about among the congregation for his wife who had arrived earlier. From my seat in the rear pew, I would point him to her location, and he thanked me by putting his hand on my shoulder as he moved in her direction. I enjoyed the touch. Along his route, he would stop and exchange pleasantries with others by whom he passed. He always said that he came to shul for the horizontal connection rather than the vertical one, and I was content to think of myself as a part of that horizontality. When I thought of him now, I saw the man whom I had desired to be my friend.

What happened?

I don't know, and I do not think I ever will, and perhaps it is *that* acknowledgment that has now made all of the difference in my hold on the world. As a result of his death—the manner of it—there rests on me now the sense that finally, we don't know anyone, and so, now, when I am engaged in conversation, and when I am inclined to say "I understand," or when people say 'they understand me,' I know that we all speak from a double ignorance: first, of the one of whom we claim to have knowledge, and second of ourselves. Really, we don't know anything at all. Nobody knows very much at all; *nobody knows*.

And all of the judgments that are made—and that I continually, even inevitably make—stem from an overwhelming ignorance. This thought gives me pause.

What happened?

Emily Dickinson says, "Because I could not stop for death/He kindly stopped for me," but perhaps a suicide *is* a kindly stopping *for* death, indeed. The last I spoke with Mark, who owned a small record label distributing high quality folk music,—two or three weeks prior—I asked him what projects were in progress, and he noted a series of new productions by original artists and several theme based compilations from the record house collections that appeared *to me* exciting and valuable. To me he had seemed enthusiastic—now I wondered what didn't I hear, for what wasn't I listening? What didn't I know? Maybe I did not detect a lack of energy in his narration. Who knows? *Nobody knows.* But then, I responded with enthusiasm and sincere interest. I was always genuinely interested in his projects. Mark, who died that Wednesday at 56 years old by his own hand, was a means of keeping records of myself, of marking my progress from the 1960's, and of staying the courses begun then in the alternative worlds we both had chosen. I think that Mark, served as my counter-cultural compass, and I flattered myself (perhaps falsely) that I kept him tuned to certain channels we shared to listen. Ironically, I had always been faithful to him, even before I knew him. In my collection, I have many of the albums produced by his company, purchased even before I knew it was Mark's company and his product. I have in my life derived great support and joy from the music he sponsored and from the traditions from which it derived and that he promoted. The music sustains me yet. Mark made his living out of his passion for music, and yet . . . it could not sustain him. How is that, I wonder? *I don't know.*

I took my seat in the last row. It is my customary seat; I am comfortable in the rear, out of the way, seeing but unseen. The Rabbis say that he who sits in the rear of the sanctuary is wicked, but Rabbi Abaye qualifies this indictment saying, "This only applies where he does not turn his face towards the Synagogue, but if he does turn his face towards the Synagogue there is no objection to it." Behind me was the coffin; I faced rigidly forward. I would not look back. I glanced steadily forward as the newly arriving mourners sought seats (what else could I call those who stop their lives in the middle of a day to attend a funeral of one who should not have yet died), and I sensed more than saw that the sides and the rear of the middle section began to fill. There were now hundreds of people already seated, and even more flowed through the doors. And yet there was barely a sound.

Sitting alone and silent in my row, I tried to imagine the overwhelming sense of pain with which Mark must have lived every moment that seemed to have led to his desire to stop living. But I could not do so. On my worst days—and yes, I have suffered through not a few of them—I have never thought my burden more than I could bear, could never bear the thought of abandoning my children and my life. He was loved, and he loved; he was successful and had the world for which to live. At least, that is what I had believed. But I did not know, nobody knows, finally, do we? And all of those people filling the room hadn't been able to help him—all of those people could offer him absolutely no support. *We could not sustain him.* What good is community, then, I wondered? What does it ever know? Or was it that despite our efforts, he could receive no succor and would not be sustained. And what good is community then? What good is community if it cannot provide comfort in those dark, dark nights? I could not begin to grasp the depth of that pain and despair, the darkness in the midst of the light, the hopelessness in the midst of all that hope that Mark must have suffered. At the heart of all of our relationships sits such ignorance.

I suppose that the dead find relief from their pain, but for me in my ignorance, I think that the greatest anguish occurs at the thought of my death. In the end, it is the dead who will not again see the sun shine, or watch the moon wax and wane. It is the dead who will not see a child's growth, or celebrate his Bar Mitzvah, or... or live a fulfilled life. The dead cannot put an arm about a child and dry the tears cried from a broken arm or a broken heart. The dead will see no more movies, hear no more songs, nor rail against the loyal opposition ever again.

Is it our own deaths we feel at funerals, is it our own fears that comprise no small part of the pain we suffer there?

The sanctuary was by now over flowingly crowded. Yet the more people who occupied the room, the deeper became its silence. We waited in dread anticipation. Suddenly, the rear door just behind me opened and the Rabbi entered, followed by the immediate family of the deceased: the wife, wailing almost uncontrollably and the terrified son, numb and trying desperately to cling to his unavailable mother. Behind them walked Mark's graying and stooped mother and father, and finally, his older sister and her family. Each wore a garment ripped to represent the rending of clothes in mourning. I didn't want to look at them.

I looked. They moved quickly enough to the first row, and sat down. Without a word or gesture, the Rabbi stepped up to the bimah. He adjusted his kippah; I think the effort served merely as something to do, a way to displace his extreme discomfort. And then he began to speak. "We are here today to perform the funeral ceremony for Mark Abrahamson. The services here will be followed by burial at Or Chadash cemetery. Following the internment, the family will begin sitting shiva at the home of his wife and his son. Shiva minyamin will be held Sunday night through Thursday at their home at 235 Merry Lane in Cleveland Shores. The family will be receiving shiva visitors during the day." Such talk seemed so cold and impersonal to me. He was finished, and we had not begun. Perhaps the sense of despair would so increase during the service that these important details might be lost if held to the conclusion.

Up to the bimah climbed Marla Goldstein who intoned in Hebrew the 23rd Psalm in its traditional melody. She wore a simple black dress, and somehow, she looked smaller than I remembered her actually being. I have listened to that psalm my whole life. In Western culture its sound and sense has become cliché. "The Lord is my shepherd, I shall not want... yea, though I walk through the shadow of the Valley of Death, I will fear no evil." But today, its melody in the Hebrew transformed the psalm into a powerful piece of dramatic poetry. Midway through the recitation, Marla's voice volubly cracked, and briefly, she paused in the recitation. Then, taking a very deep breath, she tremblingly finished.

The Rabbi stood to deliver the eulogy. "We are told that when Rabbi Johanan died, Rabbi Issac ben Eleazar began the funeral oration this way: 'Grievous is this day for Israel, As a day when the sun sets at noon.'" In my seat at the rear of the sanctuary, I thought of Dylan's statement in "Gates of Eden," where he sings of "darkness at the break of noon," but in the Rabbi's voice there was nothing sinister as I had always sensed in Dylan's, though there was something surreal about this entire event. Death, of course, is not unnatural, but like the sun setting at noon, this death was an unnatural occurrence. I had a few questions.

The Rabbi spoke warmly of Mark's life and his achievements, he spoke of Mark's family and of his great love and hope for his son, and he spoke of a recent conversation in which Mark's joy and love flowed out of him naturally. *Nobody knows.* A eulogy is meant to lament the dead in words that break the heart, but my heart was already broken. Behind me was the casket in which lay the body of a man who could no longer bear to live. What could possibly connect the stories the Rabbi narrated with the reality of what lay oppressively in the rear of the shul. One story in particular struck me. It seems that once on the beach in Miami, not long after the birth of his son, Mark had been so overcome with joy at being alive that he approached an ice cream vendor on the board walk, handed him five one hundred dollar bills and told him to give out ice cream to as many children on the beach as the money would support. A manic behavior, perhaps, but so beautifully and outwardly directed. It spoke to a sense of community, of uncontainable jubilation.

What happened? *Nobody knows.* This man, Mark Abrahamson, in the end and as an end took his own life. This man who passed out joy to hundreds and even thousands couldn't bear to live one extra minute. He hanged himself, knowing that someone he loved and who loved him would have to find him. And I guess I have been wondering what the relationship might be between the Mark Abrahamson who bought ice cream that day on the beach; the man, Mark Abrahamson, with whom I weekly conversed; and the Mark Abrahamson, who would do such a thing as hang himself. I thought that there had to be some palpable link. I demanded some connection! I had some essential questions. Was the Mark Abrahamson who we thought we knew to be loving and caring contained in the Mark Abrahamson who hanged himself? And was the Mark Abrahamson, who hanged himself, contained in the man who expressed this uncontainable love? *Ach, nobody knows.*

/lacrimoso/ I had lost track of the Rabbi's voice, but at once knew that he had concluded. He descended from the bimah, and walked over to the grieving family who sat numbly in the first row. They stood wearily and followed him up the aisle and out of the sanctuary. I sat facing forward until they had passed by me and out of the doors. The coffin had already been placed in the hungry hearse. And as the mourners stood quietly, and began to file out of the sanctuary, I began to sob volubly and uncontrollably. My face cracked, as a rock would crack from the inner pressures, and out of the new crevice water flowed. My tears fell in a steady stream, and my body shuddered in sobs.

Why was I crying? I cried for Mark who suffered so horribly; I cried for the son who had lost his father so mysteriously and so terrifyingly; and I cried for myself because Mark's death gave me the excuse to do so. I do not live in Eden, and his death served to remind me of this.

Finally, when the sanctuary was almost emptied, I stood up and turned about. I spoke to no one and no one spoke to me. I walked alone back to the coatroom and found my winter wear. I wrapped the scarf about my neck, and put the hat on my head. In my car, I waited for the cortege to start its journey to the cemetery.

≠

/*mesto*/ Who would know the hour of his death? At my daughter's college, in the Fall of 2008, a young boy went missing for several days and then was found. He had drowned in a shallow pond on his way home from a party. I ached at the loss of this lovely young life; and even now and years later I can't blot from my memory his youthful face that had been posted all over the school's website. I fear I may never feel at ease again. *Nobody knows.* I ache for his parents who in hope and love sent their child off to college and now have to bring him home. And I ached for myself as a parent whose child was off at college where she yet felt hunger, and concern for her grades, and for the progress of her social life. And where she must live her life learning to make decisions amidst shallow ponds.

Nobody knows. Dylan sings, "We live and we die, We know not why/But I'll be with you when the deal goes down." And that is supposed to be a relief. And I guess it will have to suffice, though it does not now relieve.

≠

/*mesto*/ Who would know the hour of his death?

The air was frighteningly cold even for Wisconsin. In our own vehicles, we had followed the hearse in which rested her coffin and the accompanying black limousines that carried the grieving families to the cemetery, and we now stood quietly, even patiently, in the frigid air waiting for the necessary organization to begin this last phase of the burial rites for Mrs. Kaminski who had died the day before at the age of ninety-three. Mrs. Kaminski had always claimed that she was five years younger than her actual age because as she said, "I lost five years in the Holocaust." Indeed, during the war she had been removed by the Nazis to a forced labor camp, and after three months, when she understood that she was destined for extermination at Majdenek, she managed to escape with a friend through a barbed wire fence. For the next three years, she survived living out of doors in the forests of Poland, and then for a year after the war, she was interred in a displaced person camp. Here in the Midwest, winters are impossibly cold, and every Shabbat from November to April, when my daughters and I would complain and shiver at the frigid temperatures, Mrs. Kaminski would nod her head and inevitably add, "In Poland, we lived outside all of the time. It was so cold. I don't know how I survived." It was her mantra, and I think she intoned it to remember that she was alive. Her entire family had been murdered by the Nazis and their accomplices. As Kurt Vonnegut says, "So it goes."

Now, we stood on the paved roads of the cemetery clustered about at the curb in a quiet and messy crowd behind the funeral hearse. A few automobiles were still arriving, and as each slipped almost embarrassedly to the end of the line of earlier arrivals, the occupants stepped out of their cars, quietly closed them without locking the doors, and moved along the slightly inclined road toward those of us already waiting. We nodded greetings, but offered no more. Only the sound of shuffling feet and closing car doors broke the silence. We shivered despite our winter wear, but no one spoke of the cold or of our discomfort, though we shoved our gloved hands deeply into the pockets of our winter coats, hunched our necks down into our shoulders, and pulled our hats farther down on our heads. We waited patiently to move.

When the last of the cars arrived and parked, and the mourners had all gathered into a loose crowd, the funeral directors pulled the plain pine box coffin out of the gaping rear of the hearse—and gave it over to the six pallbearers: Mrs. Kaminski's son-in-law and grandchildren, three men on either side. Mrs. Kaminski was a small woman who had gotten smaller in her aging, and I do not think that the pine box, though perhaps a burden, was at all heavy. Inside it, Mrs. Kaminski was draped and covered in her pure white shroud, her head anointed with oil. The Rabbi turned on an unmarked path through the gravestones to the newly dug site that was not yet visible to those of us still on the road. He stood unsteadily on the uneven ground. Snow and ice had not been plowed off the cemetery's informal footpaths. We instinctively and silently shuffled more closely together to follow him. We knew where we were heading though we did not yet know the exact place. Standing in front, the Rabbi began to recite the funeral liturgy from his well-worn prayer book. His nasal voice took on a rhythm at once mournful and formulaic. He was reading a passage from *Pirke Avot*. "Akavya ben Mahalalel said: 'Reflect on three things and you will avoid transgression: Know where you came from, where you are going, and before whom you will have to give an account and reckoning.'" At the moment, transgression was furthest from my thoughts. All about me was not evidence of transgression but of death. Only the living transgress; the dead in the cemetery rested silently. There was no way to know which of them had transgressed and which had lived a more blameless life. Here, were only bodies turning back into earth, and I knew, transgressing or not, I was certainly going to end up here.

≠

/tenerezza/ Despite my respect for Maimonides, I have never placed much faith in the reality of an afterlife. If an afterlife exists, it must be different from life here and would certainly not be one in which I could, like Tom and Huck, sit in the upper pews and watch my own funeral. No, the consequences for my inevitable transgression were not to be suffered in a next life; the costs had to be borne here. As some powerful superego, Akavya cautioned me about my behavior here in this life on this earth, and his standard I knew was scriptural: to care for the widow, the orphan, and the stranger in my midst because I had been a stranger myself in the land of Egypt, and God had taken me out of slavery with an outstretched arm. How that ethical life might be accomplished is the substance of Torah and is explicated in the exegetical imaginations that I have studied and continue to study extensively in that text and in the commentaries by the Rabbis throughout the years. No, in the midst of all of this death, it was of life that Akavya spoke.
/grazioso/ If all of philosophy is a footnote to Plato, perhaps it might be that all the words of Torah are a footnote to the story of Adam and Eve, their expulsion from the garden and the introduction of death into the world. Without death, there is no life, and Torah is about how to live a life. If no one died, there would be no movement and therefore, no story. If not for the death of the first born, might not the Israelites still be enslaved in Egypt? Death inspires life. Had we but world enough and time, this coyness lady were no crime; the grave's a fine and a quiet place, but none I think do there embrace, said the poet pointedly. Indeed, there is no activity in death. As an end, however, death supposes a beginning, and that beginning is always the substance of our lives. I could choose to focus only on the end. Jacob refuses to be comforted by his sons and daughter at the news of Joseph's death, crying "For, I will go down mourning to my son in Sheol," and in this story, Jacob will not again be heard from for twenty years. Or unlike Jacob, I can continue my

life despite my awareness of death. Cain slew Abel; then, Adam and Eve begot Seth. Life takes place here outside of the Garden, and that life has value because Death, too, is out here, outside of the Garden. Death need not be reckoned with, though it must be acknowledged. Though Spinoza says that the free man thinks least of all of his death, of death he must sometimes think. It is not that Spinoza didn't know about death—he did, after all, make mention of it—it is that he did not quake before it. Who would know the hour of his death? Of death Spinoza is not ignorant; indeed, he sees it well enough. After all, Spinoza spent his life grinding lenses to improve vision. Spinoza focuses on life, and therefore, devotes little time to thoughts of his death.

The High Holiday liturgy promises that repentance, prayer and charity avert the severe decree, suggesting in that formula that Death is the severest of decrees, but that it might even be circumvented by appropriate behavior. But Akavya's words are not at all about avoiding death but about answering for my life *before* it ends. Who would know the hour of his death? It is curious to me to consider that despite all of their very obvious human flaws, few in Torah ever do make such an accounting; it is we in our study of their very human lives who make account *for* them. On their death beds, Abraham, Isaac and Jacob offer blessings to their sons but make no accounting for their lives; Joseph's death is merely reported. When Pharaoh decides to let the Hebrew people go, it is not contrition that Pharaoh feels but horror. Far from accounting he makes a desperate act to end the plague. Indeed, no sooner do the deaths end than Pharaoh heads out in hot pursuit of his former slaves. Only Moses' final speeches might be considered an accounting. He narrates the entire history of the Exodus and the wanderings in the Wilderness, events in which he played, indeed, a major part. In his final speeches—can I call them Moses' accountings?—he reviews the laws and commands that God has ordained. In that recounting it is not his own transgressions of which he speaks—though he does acknowledge one or two—but refers instead to those of the people. Giving personal account does not seem central to Moses' text.

In Torah, God never seems to afford very much time for reflection and consideration. When God decides to destroy the world by flood, no time for accounting is allotted. Korah and his accomplices are swallowed up by the earth even as they stand expectantly (even hopefully) before their fire pans. These Biblical figures die without accounting for their lives. Before his death, Joshua makes a covenant with the people, but I don't think such a deal is what Akavya has in mind.

David uses his deathbed confession to demand revenge be exacted on his enemies, and of Solomon, it is simply reported that he died. Jesus makes no final accounting for his life, though he does forgive those who knew exactly what they did. These persons live, and then they die, and except perhaps for Moses, they make no final accounting. If Akavya suggests that there is someone to whom accounting must be made, then Torah suggests it is my fellow humans to whom attention must be paid. In our time, the Rabbis and scholars who interpret the laws by which my life might be defined have substituted Akavya's God with my superego. And as I look about me in this graveyard, I do not know what accounting to make. Except for us, in this cemetery there is nobody here!

/mesto/ Actually, Akavya wasn't through. He proceeded to particularize his own counsel. The Rabbi stood facing into the heart of the cemetery and continued with Akavya's words: "'Where you came from' —from a putrid drop." I had never heard that before, and I experienced a profound shock at the idea. I considered this statement a rather phallocentric and appalling perspective on procreation, situating our origin in decay: I had always thought better of my semen and the reproductive process. Akavya continued, but his perspective offered no relief: "'Where are you going' —to a place of dust, worms and maggots." And ah, yes, I've come round to that opinion myself. *Genesis* and my life remind me, "By the sweat of your brow shall you get bread to eat, Until you return to the ground—For from it you were taken." The bottom of the pine box coffin that held the body of Mrs. Kaminski had holes drilled in it to allow the earth to sooner work on the body so that it would return sooner back to the earth. And then, Akavya's final answer: "And before whom you will have to give an account and reckoning—before the Supreme King of kings, the Holy One, blessed be He." Here is the great superego externalized, though I think that accounting and reckoning here and now is sufficient. Once dead I am beyond consequence. I am reminded again of Spinoza: to live freely—which is to live rationally and responsibly—requires neither accounting nor reckoning. The story is told that one evening Spinoza left the dinner table in the home where he kept a rented room, climbed upstairs, lay down on his bed, and died peacefully, his great book, *Ethics*, unpublished and his work unfinished. Death always comes too soon and immortality too late.

To avoid transgression is to step into ethics, and Akavya's standard remained a high one, indeed. Akavya suggests that it is God before whom I must make account, but the absent face of God into which I would look returns me to my own face and that of the widow, the orphan and the stranger in my midst. Perhaps character is determined by an ability to continue to live despite repeated failures to attain this ethical standard. It appears to me that my actions here are almost immediately accounted for one way or another, and it is always myself before whom I must give report and reckoning. Akavya was suggesting that knowledge of my past and my ultimate future— death—would keep my present self from transgression.

/patetico/ Where did I come from? The more I learn, the more I create my origins, but where I ultimately came from I will never definitively know. I could secularize this dictum and give it materialist foundations. An acquired predilection to historicize everything demands a studied consideration of my present standing. I am, in fact, obsessed with origins. I may not always know exactly where I am, but I have spent many fruitful years in libraries and therapy studying some interesting possibilities whence I came, and have often considered (sometimes with horror and sometimes with amusement) the ingenious attempts in which I have engaged to obfuscate these origins. There are any number of methods I employed—and continue to employ—to both consider and to avoid considering the nature of my responsibilities—I have spent enough years reading Freud, Lacan, Winnicott and even Marx to acknowledge this truth—and even a casual study of my behavior would reveal the strategies in which I engage to maintain my ignorance even when the consequences of my behavior stand immediately before me.

Where I am going? If I actually knew that, I probably wouldn't go there, opposed as I am to all traces of determinism and predestination. Death is not where I go, but what will come to me. Before whom must I make accounting? Myself, of course, but the standards I might use for this accounting send me back to the question from where I came. Fortunately, Akavya's admonition insists that I live in the present. Somewhere, a more optimistic Rabbi said that I am not required to complete the task, but neither am I permitted to abandon it. At present, all I can ever say is, I'm not finished. But what kind of accounting is that? As I followed her coffin, I knew that Mrs. Kaminski's task was now done, and we were now gathered to bury her. As we stood amidst the tombstones, I thought about *Waiting for Godot*. Vladimir says to Estragon, "Nothing to be done," and the latter responds, "I'm coming round to that opinion myself." The more years I live, the less I have available. Death always comes too soon and immortality too late.

No, Akavya's words are not about death but about life. I'm beginning to think there is nothing to be said about Death, though certainly it is a major topic in our lives.

/*mesto*/ The Rabbi stepped forward and began the short passage to the grave. He walked precariously over the snow toward the gravesite on some unmarked path through the tombstones and began to intone Psalm 91, the traditional psalm read in the cemetery at Jewish funerals. We followed silently behind, led by the words. It is a curious psalm to read at the cemetery as the coffin is carried to its gravesite. "He who lives in the shelter of the Most High dwells in the shadow of the Almighty. I say of the Lord, my Refuge and Stronghold, my God in whom I trust, that He will save you from the fowler's snare and the deadly pestilence. With his pinions He will cover you and beneath His wings you will find shelter. His faithfulness is an encircling shield." Curiously enough, it is to the living to whom this psalm is addressed. As we walk toward the open earth into which we will lay Mrs. Kaminski, we are comforted that we are subject to God's protection. She, however, is beyond anyone's care. I assume that to live in the shelter of the Most High refers to a life that is bounded by the commandments; to live an ethical life is to gain God's protection. Or does the psalm suggest that it is enough merely to maintain a belief in God's protective power that guarantees my safety and an avoidance of *unnatural* death? Death is otherwise inevitable.

I think a child's faith in the endless and enduring protective care of the parent is expressed here, a belief that the whole of history denies. Cain's irrational murder of his brother is only the first of too many senseless massacres of those who lived under the shelter of the Most High. But perhaps surrounded as we are here in the cemetery by evidence of so much death, the psalm means to offer some comfort to those who have not strayed from out of the shelter of God's minions. Of course, shelter serves a double purpose here. On the one hand, it seems to refer to the commandments, but on the other hand, it means the protection of God's great wings. The world is harsh and dangerous outside of the Garden, and we are subject to human and natural danger that might cut short our lives, but here, in the psalm, we are assured that if we stay protected in God's shadow, we may remain safe. I think about the deceptive shadows in Plato's cave, and I wonder.

/*lacrimoso*/ The Rabbi paused in his walking, for who would be anxious to bring anyone to the grave. We do not hurry in this task, though we cannot question its necessity. Behind the Rabbi, the loosely assembled people, too, ceased to advance, though some in the congregation had not yet even reached the unmarked snow-covered path to the gravesite. Many people had traveled to the cemetery to help bury

Mrs. Kaminski. My eyes remained on the coffin that did not halt in its movement. It was we, the living, who were reticent to move forward. The Rabbi read, "You need not fear terror by night, nor the arrow that flies by day; not the pestilence that stalks in darkness nor the plague that ravages at noon. A thousand may fall at your side, ten thousand at your right hand, but it will not come near you. You will only look with your eyes and see the punishment of the wicked."

Who would know the hour of their death? This psalm promises that though violent death surrounds me, so long as I remain faithful to the shelter of the Most High it will not approach me. In a violent and dangerous world, I am safe from violence and danger. In the peace of this cemetery, I find resonance in these words, but not 200 yards behind me the world lies in wait, and out there, a car horn blares. I do not believe the words of the psalm; its denial speaks a childish belief. The psalm assures me that in God's shadow dwell not the violent and unnatural, and that there I am safe from violent and unnatural Death. The psalm promises just punishment for the wicked, but my experience leads me to a different conclusion. I know that the reach of the wicked is too long, that too often the rewards of sin are great, and the innocent too often suffer an unnatural and violent death. The death of the children during the Holocaust is a case in point. Mrs. Kaminski, at least, lived her fourscore years plus ten. Perhaps the psalm suggests that as long as I focus on the life ethically lived, the less I will experience fear. This reading is Spinoza's.

The Rabbi moved forward again, and he continued with the prayer. "Because you said 'The Lord is my Refuge' taking the Most High as your shelter, no harm will befall you, no plague will come near your tent, for He will command His angels about you, to guard you in your ways. They will lift you in their hands, lest your foot stumble on a stone. You will tread on lions and vipers, you will trample on young lions and snakes." Honestly, I don't recall ever speaking these words, but I know that accompanying the corpse to its grave does honor to the living, and so perhaps my actions do sometimes speak louder than my words. But now the cadence of the psalm served as a type of charm as I walked through the cemetery. Here was Death but no danger. Following the coffin, I was being assured that I was safe despite my surroundings.

Again the Rabbi stopped. And behind him we shoved our hands more deeply into our pockets, hunched more tightly our shoulders, and watched the coffin in front of us. Formerly in Judea, no fewer than seven halts and sit-downs were ordained in escorting the dead. This custom derives from a reading of *Ecclesiastes* where it says "Vanity of vanities, says Koheleth; vanity of vanities, all is vanity." The singular forms of the word, vanity, are added to the two plural instances to equal seven. The Rabbis have spent considerable energy to mandate each detail of the funeral, and to ensure that each individual receives a proper burial. But it is really the living with whom these Rabbis seem concerned. At one time the cost of a funeral was so exorbitant that the poor would just leave the bodies of their dead and run away. Thus, Rabbi Gamaliel II in the first century ordered that at his death he be dressed in only inexpensive linen shrouds, and from that time on, all the people followed his lead. Obviously, the dead do not care in what they are clothed, but Gamaliel was concerned with the feelings of the living. All of these mandates are for the living, including the prescriptions for the post funeral meal (to rich and poor alike the food is brought in baskets of peeled willow shoots), and for the drinks to be served (in the homes of rich and poor alike the glass must be colored). It is the living who demand attention. Indeed, it is they who must keep on keeping on. The symbolisms and rituals of the funeral and the periods of mourning must finally come to an end. We learn, "Our masters taught, There are three things God reluctantly thought of, but even if He had not thought of them, they had to be thought of: that a corpse should smell foul, that the dead should be put out of mind, and that produce should rot." I appreciate that the Rabbis ascribe reluctance to God's actions: God soon realized that without Death there would no life, but that Death was not a consummation devoutly to be wished. The first thing of which God makes certain is that the family not keep the body about; the second that death does not end all life, and the third that the speculators not hold out for higher prices. No, the Rabbis were certainly fixed on the living. All of this order ensures that the living get over the dead.

A dozen yards ahead was the gravesite. The Rabbi moved forward and spoke again. "God says, Because he loves me, I will rescue him; I will protect him, because he acknowledges My name. When he calls on me, I will answer him. I will be with him in distress, I will deliver him and bring him honor. With long life I will satisfy him, and show him my salvation. With long life I will satisfy him, and show him my salvation." The contingency of God's love is the fear of every child: how much must I love before I am loved in return and deserving of God's protection. I appreciate the repetitive final line; I am reassured by its emphasis though I am not necessarily comforted. Death always comes too soon and immortality too late.

Of course, according to the psalm my salvation is again contingent: *if* I love God, acknowledge God's sovereignty, and my need for

God, *then* I am guaranteed God's protection from dishonor, from silence and from early death. But these conditions also are about life and not about death, for to love and acknowledge a faceless, even Absent Deity, requires that I look into the face of the widow, the orphan and the stranger in my midst. And they are all about me on this trek to the grave. The meaning of the funeral rests in the life it requires. The Rabbi ceased his inevitable march again.

◢

/*expressivo*/ Death itself is only final. The nothingness of death provokes its association with Evil, but Death itself is not Evil. Indeed, without Death there would exist no motive to act: we would live as lotus eaters. Out here away from Eden might be work, pains and illness, out here might be where decisions must be made. Out here might be suffering and death, but out here is where something can be done. Out here is life. While I live, I continue to fall upon the thorns of life and bleed, and I welcome the opportunities. When I die, I will cease to fall and to bleed. I hate not that Death exists, but that it is not life. Who would know the hour of his death?

/*affectuoso*/ As for myself, I've got an enlarged aorta, a euphemism for an aortic aneurysm. It could kill me at any time. Apparently, I've had this condition for several years. It may have grown more serious recently, but no one can really answer that question. Unlike a tree, there are no rings in my aorta to measure annual growth. In fact, the condition was discovered in a CT scan ordered for an issue wholly unrelated to my heart, and were it not for the pulmonary concern requiring the scan, I would not know that I had an enlarged aorta, nor the bicuspid aortic valve that a transesophogeal echocardiogram revealed. I would have remained innocent of inevasible mortality. But a moment occurred when suddenly the reality of death turned from a theoretical construct to a real and even imminent possibility. That awareness of death then became a permanent lens through which I must forever see the world; cognizance of my mortality altered completely the way I existed in the world. I no longer held the illusory hope of a return to the innocence of the Garden: by the sweat of your brow you will earn your bread until you return to the ground. I have experienced that moment.

In my life, I had been relatively healthy. Whenever I became sick, I got well, sometimes all by myself and at other times, as a result of some prescribed medication. But always, I returned to health and to my running. Now, I have a condition, an enlarged aorta, for which there is treatment but no cure. The medications I take now preventative and meant to keep the aneurysm from worsening and the aorta from tearing apart. At some moment, in a not distant future I may undergo an operation to replace my valves. I am hopeful. But Yossarian's panicked cry that every cell in his body is waiting to turn traitor has become not at all amusing. I live now knowing all too well that I will die. If it be not now, yet it will come. Regardless. A free man thinks least of all his death. Who would know the hour of his death!

There have been earlier hints of mortality. Several years ago, I broke my ankle. I was out running with Gary, my road companion of twenty years, and I slipped on the ice, upended, and came down somehow with a foot twisted horridly awry. Without thinking, I twisted it back, as if I had merely to screw the foot back on to repair the damage. Alas, I had no success there. Gary ran back to the car in what he claims to be his fastest mile ever, drove too quickly I am sure back to where I was lying despairingly on the ice, packed me moaning into the front seat, and sped to the hospital. By the time we arrived at the emergency room, there was a swelling the size of a tennis ball on the inside of my right ankle.

Interestingly, I did not immediately suffer any great pain: some said it was the endorphins, others said it was psychic numbing. Even when I tried to turn my foot aright, I felt nothing. I lay there anguished that there would be no more running for some time, and I could not imagine how I would psychically survive the abrupt cessation. I had been running for thirty years, and had never rested for more than four days consecutively, never paused longer than those four days from taking my thoughts and my troubles out on the road. I now envisioned too many troubled months ahead. I decided to schedule an appointment with a psychotherapist.

I had to have surgery on the ankle, during which they placed pins and plates and other implements of construction into the bones. I hoped to be back on the roads with Gary twelve weeks later, but in the meantime, I felt like a hobbling cliché.

Now, I could hardly move. Every event had to be carefully planned. Whereas before I was completely mobile, now I was completely immobile. I could not get up from my chair to get an extra pencil, to find a book from the shelf, to urinate at will. I could not carry my laptop computer about with me, nor plug it in to what had now become a very inconvenient outlet. I could not arise from my labors easily to make another cup of coffee—not because I could not get to the stove, (though it was certainly a chore to maneuver there), but because I could not return to my desk in Walden using my crutches and carrying the filled cup as well. I found myself imagining such inventions as crutch-hooks onto which one could hang things like filled coffee mugs, slices of French bread and apples, leaving my hands free to facilitate travel on the crutches. Suddenly, the world had to be rethought and reorganized from the position of immobility. For example, sitting on the downstairs couch—it made no sense to go upstairs until it was absolutely necessary. I might need to use the bathroom, but to do so would require the expense of energy to arise up out of my chair, move the computer off of my lap and find some temporary resting place for it, reach for my crutches, lift myself out of my chair, schlep myself to the toilet—for ease onto which I would sit—and then schlep myself back to my chair, opening assorted doors along the way. It was much easier to stay in my chair, albeit, a bit uncomfortable. If I waited just a few minutes, then I might use the return trip from the bathroom to grab some breakfast in the kitchen through which I must pass to return to my seat. Conservation of energy.

And whereas I once thought myself completely independent, suddenly I had become wholly dependent. Oh, I do not mean to exaggerate, nor even romanticize—even though I still hobbled about on crutches, I yet controlled all of my bodily functions and I maintained all of my F-A-C-U-L-T-I-E-S. But I could not, as the cliché goes, walk and chew gum at the same time. I could move on crutches into the next room, but I could not also carry my book along with me. I could still enjoy a large cone of Ben & Jerry's ice cream, but not while I tottered shakily down the street.

So many unassuming acts now required assumption. And so, for the first time in my entire life, I was forced to rest wholly and completely. I could not run, and I could not walk. I could not drive. I could not cook, and I could not clean. I was consigned to my chair and to my books. I was confined to immobility. Oddly enough, there was some privileged sense of freedom in that restriction.

And as I healed, I wondered whether I could really just move back into the life that had so abruptly stopped those many weeks ago when my ankle broke? How could I ever move back into the life without the memory of breaking the ankle? As Dylan writes, "I used to care, but things have changed." I longed for that moment when I could walk unassumingly and without a limp. I anticipated the time when I need not calculate every move so as to accomplish my purpose with greatest conservation of energy. I could not wait to give up my crutches. I wanted once again to run on the roads. I wanted to be young again!

But I had broken my ankle, and I could no longer live without that memory. Actually, I used *not* to care, but things had changed. I could not forget. I had tasted mortality, and it was not to my liking. I established some new cautions: I would be very vigilant when I was around ice—frozen water—and I would no longer be so cavalier about my steadiness of foot. Now, I am more conscious of the earth's subtle undulations; I feel the slightest depression.

[pesante] The idea of death as 'no more' I find incomprehensible. Someone dies, and they lie as if asleep, but they will not awaken. Having always awakened from my sleep, I cannot imagine what not to awaken must be like. Of course, this wonder implies a consciousness of not waking, and the dead do not possess such capacity, I think. The dead do not dream, I believe. The dead do not feel, though the Rabbis are not firm on this opinion. Some say that they can only feel the sufferings of the living, and others deny even this sentience. Perhaps it is that the dead do not even know that they *are* dead. We are only a too, too solid flesh and that is all, soon to melt, thaw and resolve itself into a dew. The Rabbis say that "When the soul leaves the body, its cry [of anguish] goes from one end of the world to the other." Dust to dust. But having acted always with consciousness, I cannot imagine the absence of everything that is Death. No more. Nothing. Absolute nothingness without even the realization of the nothingness. The notion appalls more that it frightens, though it frightens, of course, by a complete absence of credibility.

The Torah refers to death as a return to kin; death here is portrayed as some kind of homecoming. Hamlet calls it an undiscovered country from whose bourn no traveler returns. Death is a place. "Rage, rage against the dying of the light," Dylan Thomas urges his father. Death is a darkness. Sometimes death is portrayed as a brilliant pure light, blinding illumination. Death, where is thy sting: death is a poisonous creature inflicting pain and suffering, though ironically the suffering of the dying is often relieved by death. It is the living who feel death's sting. Death be not proud: death is personified as a vain and unworthy human.

[lamentoso] Clearly, death is all around me, but I understand it none the more because it is so proximate. I am familiar with its presence

but fail to comprehend it. It is non-being, and this makes no sense to being. Who would know the hour of his death? Koheleth cautions, "For the time of mischance comes to all. And a man cannot even know his time. As fishes are enmeshed in a fatal net, and as birds are trapped in a snare, so men are caught at the time of calamity, when it comes upon them without warning." "Mischance" and "the time of calamity" are the Rabbis' euphemisms for death; even the wise Solomon had difficulty speaking the term itself. And though I am relieved by his reticence, I am not comforted that Solomon the wise understood death in such negative terms. The Sixties philosophy which I daily breathed taught me that today was the first day of the rest of my life, but the Rabbis say here to treat every day as if it were my last. I suppose there is some coincidence between these two positions: if I live every day as the first day of the rest of my life, then everything is possible; but if today is my last day, then today everything is possible. Who would know the hour of his death? The Rabbis anticipated this ignorance: they suggest that the reason we are not given the hour of our death is to prevent us from lying abed awaiting it; they mean us to be up and about our doing. All is possible. Death is of course inevitable, even imminent, but its imminence should not deter us from living. Spinoza, (again) said that the free man thinks least of all of his death.

/grazioso/ Who would know the hour of his death? Aaron and Moses do come to such knowledge, though unlike the suicide, they do not choose it; as like for so many of us, the moment is chosen for them by God. And there is little discrepant time between the announcement and the death. Up until their deaths, Aaron and Moses are about and doing. First, Aaron:

> /mesto/ At Mount Hor, on the boundary of the land of Edom, the Lord said to Moses and Aaron, 'Let Aaron be gathered to his kin: he is not to enter the land that I have assigned to the Israelite people, because you disobeyed my command about the waters of Meribah. Take Aaron and his son Eleazar and bring them up on Mount Hor. Strip Aaron of his vestments and put them on his son Eleazar. Then Aaron shall be gathered unto the dead."

> Moses did as the Lord commanded. They ascended Mount Hor in the

sight of the whole community. Moses stripped Aaron of his vestments and put them on his son Eleazar, and Aaron died there on the summit of the mountain.

/grazioso/ To my mind, this is the first death in Torah that is formally announced. Usually, Torah records that the person has reached a considerable age and will soon be, euphemistically, called to his kin. Interestingly, it is only the men who are so called; for the women of the Torah, a simple sentence announcing their death is recorded, though even this simple notice is sometimes lacking. Death seems to take the women wholly by surprise, and they experience it alone. Of Sarah and Leah, we are told simply that they have died and been buried in the cave of Machpelach; of Rebekah's death, there is no record at all in Torah. The Rabbis explain that Rebekah was buried at night because every holy person who might walk before her bier was either dead or absent. Isaac, her husband, the Rabbis say, was too blind and weak to assist in her burial, and the Rabbis refused to permit Esau to return home to walk before the coffin of his mother. "Should wicked Esau walk before her bier, people will say, 'A curse on the breast that gave suck to such a one.'" We must never speak ill of the dead who cannot defend themselves. The last matriarch, Rachel, dies giving birth to her last child, and though her last words name that child Ben-Yoni, which means 'son of my sorrow,' upon her death Jacob renames the child Benjamin, child of strength. So much for women's initiative.

Aaron's death seems the most carefully plotted demise in Torah. Interestingly, in Torah the announcement is made to both Moses *and* Aaron, but the legends that have arisen suggest that Aaron is not immediately privy to this information. The stories suggest that it is only Moses whom God informs of his brother's impending Death, and that Moses is very uncomfortable following God's directions. I am not sure why the Rabbis would vary the story so significantly. The brothers had, along with their sister Miriam, who herself had recently died in the desert, but of whose burial there is no report, led the people out of Egypt and through the wilderness. The death of Aaron now will leave Moses alone. Although Moses has a wife and children, his role as leader has estranged him from them. Moses essentially has no family. Or rather, everyone is family to Moses.

On the day of Aaron's death, the story goes, Moses came to Aaron and aroused him from his sleep. When Aaron asked why Moses had arrived so early, Moses suggested that he had been thinking of Torah and had yet a few questions, especially about the first book,

Genesis. Aaron was the High Priest, and though it was Moses who heard the word of God, the Rabbis suggest that Moses here showed respect for Aaron's learning. Moses spoke to his older brother (Aaron is 123 years old) of all that God had created and how good had been Creation. Moses then asked his brother, what could be said of Adam who brought death into the world, such that even you and I must come to a like end. How clever Moses seems, by indirection to find direction out.

I suspect Aaron must have wondered at the tenor of the conversation and might have even asked his brother how it was that Moses would raised now the idea of their deaths when there was yet so much to do. Indeed, Aaron might have said that actually he felt quite healthy, thank you. And Moses pointedly and even poignantly answered his brother that despite Aaron's apparent rigor, God had actually decreed his death and assigned to Moses the responsibility of burying Aaron and the transference of the robes of the High Priest to Aaron's oldest son, Eleazar. The midrash says that Aaron was crushed. "My heart writhes within me; and the terrors of death are fallen upon me," quoting from *Psalms*, that, of course, had not yet been written. What those terrors might be Torah never suggests. As I have said, death in Torah is just the end of life, no more. Nonetheless, Aaron acceded to God's command, (what choice did he ever have?) and according to God's directions, ascended Mount Hor with Moses and Eleazar. When they arrived at the top of the mountain, the story goes, a cave opened up and inside of it was a burning lamp and a couch that had been made by an angel in Heaven. Aaron removed his garments one by one and placed each on his son. In Torah, Moses dresses Eleazar in his father Aaron's robes. But perhaps the Rabbis intend to parallel here the transference of the holy garments to Eleazar with the blessings Abraham, Isaac and Jacob gave to their sons; each of these acts serve as an appropriate frame to a consecrated and dedicated life. Then, Moses consoled his brother that at least Aaron and Miriam had someone to attend their funeral, whereas he, Moses, would have no kin left to bury him. In these thoughts of his own death, Moses already reveals regret for the life he had chosen. Then, Moses told Aaron to lie upon the couch. "Stretch out your arms," and Aaron stretched them out. "Shut your eyes," and Aaron shut them. "Close your mouth," and Aaron closed it. At once, the Presence came down, and as it kissed him, Aaron's soul departed. Then, as Moses and Eleazar kissed him on his cheeks, the cloud of glory rose up and covered Aaron. The Holy One commanded Moses and Eleazar, "Go hence." The moment they left, the cave was sealed. And the people wept for Aaron for thirty days. Death is a sleep.

Not long after Aaron's burial, God tells Moses that he, too, must soon die, but before he is called to his ancestors, there is still much he must do. Moses' last days are to be full: he completes the writing of Torah that must be "read aloud in the presence of all Israel." Moses instructs Joshua, who will lead the Israelites upon Moses' death, to be strong and resolute, and cautions him that the people he will lead are stubborn and stiff-necked; his leadership will not be an easy one. Then, on God's command, Moses writes down the final poem "which may be my witness against the people of Israel . . . For I know what plans they are devising even now, before I bring them onto the land that I promised on oath." It is not an accounting of his life, but a warning, even a denunciation of the people. Moses proceeds to teach this poem to the Israelites.

Though Moses admits that he is old and 'can no longer be active,' he prepares for his demise with precision. He makes sure that Joshua is assigned as leader and that the Torah (the Teaching) will be read aloud to the people at least once every year. God then calls Moses and Joshua to the Tent of Meeting so that God can instruct Joshua as to his responsibilities. It is said that Moses asked Joshua what God had said to him, but Joshua responded that when God had spoken to Moses he had not shared any of that conversation with Joshua. Death is an isolation. Moses then offers his blessing to the people of each of the twelve tribes. Finally, Moses climbs the mountain where he is able to see the entire land God had promised to the Israelites, and "so Moses the servant of the Lord died there, in the land of Moab, at the command of the Lord. He buried him in the valley in the land of Moab, near Beth-peor; and no one knows his burial place to this day. Moses was a hundred and twenty years old when he died; his eyes were undimmed and his vigor unabated." Moses' last days are, as I said, quite full, and even though he himself recognizes his lack of vigor, Torah, at least, refuses to acknowledge his weariness.

Nevertheless, there is a long midrash that recounts how, at the end of his life, Moses attempts to bargain with God for his life. Cessation does not appeal to him, it would seem. First, Moses draws a circle about himself, and standing within it, prays that the severe decree be averted, but God commands that Moses' prayer be not brought to him. Having failed in his first attempt, Moses asks God to allow him to enter the land at least as a dead body, even as his ancestor Joseph will enter it, the bones of the latter having been carried about in the forty years of wandering in the wilderness to be buried at Shechem, where Joseph's grave would become a heritage. But God again refuses, claiming that Joseph had never denied being a Hebrew (a question-able claim I would say, no evidence that I can discover exists that he ever acknowledged being a Hebrew, either, at least until he reveals himself to his brothers and brings his father to Egypt) but that Moses denied his identity when he returned from Midian. Then, Moses asks God at least to allow him to live in the Promised Land "like a beast of the field . . . like a bird that flies in every direction to gather its food and in the evening returns to its nest," but again God refuses. There is in the end no negotiating with Death's imminence.

/morendo/ Moses appears desperate; despite his very long and difficult life, he will not give it up. Unlike his brother and sister, he will not go gently into that good night. Finally, Moses approaches each of the heavenly bodies to plead for him, but each claims its own vulnerabil-ity and would plead first for itself. Moses exclaims, "Shall the feet that once walked on Holy Ground, now be brought to dust?"

And God's response is ultimate: "That was my thought [from the very beginning], and such must be the way of the world: each genera-tion is to have its own providers, each generation is to have its own leaders." From the very beginning of time, Moses was meant to die to make room for the next set of leaders. We were born to die. Death serves life here. But it is still death. And it is still a loss. Who would know the hour of their death?

What is it about this knowledge that makes it so frightening? As soon as Moses learns of his impending Death, he grows afraid. And yet without death what is life? This knowledge of my enlarged aorta ought not to be where life begins. Or should it? Certainly, death's reality defines some definite border to my life that I understand now will not go on forever. This aortic enlargement of which I have learned in just the recent past is in a stage right now that is hardly life threatening and may not require any attention for another several years, but somewhere down the line, I will bargain for my life, and someone may open up my chest and fix my heart! Ironically, a repair to my heart is what I have sought for years, though then it did not include physical surgery.

Doesn't this closeness of death begin a new perspective on my life in which my mortality will play a greater part and have more influence.

In a few steps, the Rabbi stood at the base of the gaping hole. He waited while the family gathered opposite him under the green canvas canopy erected to protect them from the elements. The rest of us gathered irregularly about the site, closing a circle around the gravesite.

/*mesto*/ Ripping up the earth to create this home (Home is what I must leave in order to go anywhere though never to arrive. Home is from where I depart from those whom I know and go to those whom I will leave) had left the earth uneven and made standing unsteady. The sun shone brilliantly, though the crisp, cold winter air chilled the mourners gathering about the grave site. Mrs. Kaminski's coffin was placed atop the grave on straps attached to a metal frame, and after it rested steadily, the funeral director who dressed in a black suit, and an African-American cemetery worker attired in navy blue uniformed work clothes, pulled on the straps and the pulley system lowered the bare coffin into the empty hole. The mechanical squeaks and strains and clangings of the process intruded upon the stillness of the moment, and seemed offensive. In less than a quarter of a minute, the coffin lay securely and unseen at the bottom of the hole. The straps were pulled up, and the metal frame removed. Then, the director and the cemetery worker moved away from the site and stood respectfully a dozen or so yards away. Our eyes remained fixed on the gaping black hole in the earth into which Mrs. Kaminski's coffin had been lowered. Dust to dust.

Prayer book in hand, the Rabbi began to intone in Hebrew the Acceptance of the Judgment—the traditional prayer that declares the acceptance by the living of the judgment that is Death. Mrs. Kaminski, of course, had already accepted her Death, and though the Rabbi spoke to the open hole, his words were addressed to us who surrounded her grave. "The Rock, His work is perfect, for all His ways are just; A faithful God who does no wrong, righteous and far is He. The Rock, perfect in every deed..." Death, a perfect and just act, occurs in a world overseen by One who is perfect and *ipso facto*, death is perfectly just. Mrs. Kaminski, far from perfect, had been brought in her Death to perfection by her perfect God. Yet, Mrs. Kaminski would never be aware of this knowledge. I wondered what could possibly be so perfect about Death. Certainly, I suppose, that it is final. Indeed, one meaning of the word 'perfect' means to be completely corresponding to a definition, pattern or description. When we die, there is nothing more that can be done: there is nothing to be done. Death is perfect because *it* cannot change, nor does it permit any further change. Death is perfect because it is nothing but what it is. Death is not about finish but about end although we might remember that there is still the turn to dust that is included in the meaning of death. Death means nothing more to be done.

Perhaps perfect can define the state proper to anything when completed. Death is perfect in its completion. It terminates life irrevocably even if that particular life is not complete. And this completion does not mean that a life has been completely lived, but only that it is completely ended. There is no judgment of the value of any particular life suggested here. Death is perfect because it is the work of God who is perfect.

/maestoso/ The perfection of Death in this prayer speaks to its completion.

/grazioso/ What is also perfect about Death is that it is absolute. Death fully answers to that which its name implies, the termination of life. Freud talks about the death drive, but he speaks only of the force and not the thing itself. We can live with the death drive, but we cannot live once we have died. Death's end is absolute, and though resurrectionists and reincarnationists claim there is still life to come, it is the nature of our lives here that they use to define that bourn from which no traveler has ever really returned. Our unwillingness to accept the absoluteness of death invents that afterlife, and our terror of death's absoluteness keeps us alive. Though Keats professes to be half in love with easeful death in "Ode to a Nightingale," he does not drink the palliative that would ease him into that death, but rather, takes his ease on the escapist wings of Poesy. Keats knows that to die is to become a sod, and as much as he would "Fade far away, dissolve, and quite forget/. . . The weariness, the fever, and the fret/Here, where men sit and hear each other groan;/ Where palsy shakes a few, sad, last gray hairs,/Where youth grows pale, and spectre-thin, and dies;/Where but to think is to be full of sorrow/And leaden-eyed despairs,/Where Beauty cannot keep her lustrous eyes,/Or new Love pine at them beyond to-morrow," Keats would not really die, though for him it might be pretty to think so. To Keats, death seems a welcome—even romantic—end, though perhaps it is finally, too final.

So too, for Macbeth, in fact. At the end of his life, Macbeth assumes no responsibility for it: "life is a tale told by an idiot full of sound and fury and signifying nothing." His dusty death is the inevitable end of his meaningless life, and though death may seemingly end the absurdity, there is still the life-to-come over which Macbeth cannot jump. He has sought a world without consequence, but such is not the character of this one here. And though to him life is meaningless, ironically, he chooses to fight to the death to preserve it rather than at the end to fall upon his sword.

/*maestoso*/ I think the perfection of death in this prayer speaks to its absolute finality.

And when something is perfect, it is in a state of complete excellence and therefore, flawless. What is so flawless about death is exactly its finality and its completion. In a world of the contingent, the evanescent, and the uncertain, death is undeniably absolute. About Death there is no blemish. It is wholly what it is, no more and no less, the absolute end of life here on earth. Those of us who stood around the gravesite in accepting Mrs. Kaminski's death accepted it as just and as final, even if we did not absolutely believe it was right. There are many we must bury, and there is one that God buried, and we are certain we shall never see the like of either again.

/*maestoso*/ I think the perfection of death in this prayer speaks to its flawlessness.

The Rabbi continued: "Who can say to Him, What have you done? He rules below and above, He brings death and gives life, bringing down to the grave and raising up again. The Rock—perfect in every deed. Who can say to Him, Why do you so act? You who speak and act: show us kindness we do not deserve, and in the merit of the one who was bound like a lamb, hear us and act," I recognize the allusion to the binding of Isaac here, a subject I have long considered. I am, after all, a son. I had a father. I have a son. Isaac's merit inheres in his willingness to be bound and sacrificed, and in this submissiveness rests his strength. Indeed, this passivity characterizes his entire life. This prayer speaks not of Abraham's faith but of Isaac's acceptance, which is not exactly equivalent to faith. Here in this cemetery it is not faith we require so much as acceptance of the judgment, which I suppose *is* faith. As Isaac did not question his father's intention, neither must we question the death of her whom we now bury. We stand before this grave, and we accept the judgment of death.

But I wonder if our acceptance of the judgment here isn't radically different than that of Isaac. After all, it was he who was going to die, and we are going to exit the cemetery when these obsequies were all finished. We will wash our hands before exiting the place, wash the dirt from our hands and become clean again, as if death were contagious like the common cold. On Mt. Moriah, Isaac did not plead for his life, but in this prayer, we ask God to hear us and to act for us.

What else could we say but let us live another day! This would be the kindness for which we appeal to God: continued life. In the midst of all of this death, we ask for life. Superficially, these phrases appear as a type of charm to help us get out of the cemetery alive: hear us here and act, we implore. Cemeteries are not welcome places. /pesante/ I am reminded of Juliet's fears.

> How if, when I am laid into the tomb,
> I wake before that time that Romeo
> Comes to redeem me . . . Shall I not then be stifled in the vault
> To whose foul mouth no healthsome air breathes in,
> And there lie strangled ere my Romeo comes?

Juliet fears she might too early awaken and surrounded by death, go mad – or even, in her rage, desecrate the bodies and murder herself with their bones. Only drinking the potion given her by Friar Laurence calms her. So, too, here in the cemetery, we ask for comfort. Show us kindness that we do not deserve. Protect us here and now, we ask. We would be out of this place.

/mesto/ But if we are artlessly pleading to be spared death, then what we ask is not possible. Here, I think of Kuhn at Auschwitz, who is for a day spared selection and prays fervently to God for having saved him. Levi writes, "Does Kuhn not understand that what has happened today is an abomination, which no propitiatory prayer, no pardon, no expiation by the guilty, which nothing at all in the power of man can ever clean again. If I was God, I would spit at Kuhn's prayer!" There are no circumstances in which our prayer will spare us from death: "if it be now, tis not to come; if it be not to come, it will be now; if it be not now, yet it will come: the readiness is all."

"Repent one day before your death. Let your clothes always be freshly washed, your head never lack ointment." A free man thinks least of all of his death, though we are not ever spared from death. The prayer asks for a kindness that is not an avoidance of death, but appears a request for a deferment from it. The prayer contains no question of the justice of God's ways, though I must acknowledge that the repetition in these lines suggests at least some sense of unease. In our sorrow, we wonder about the judgment, but in our faith, we must not doubt. Yea, though we walk through the valley of the shadow of death, may we fear no evil. There is also the hint in these lines of some hope of resurrection: the reference to bringing down to the grave and rising up again. Here, the raising of the dead is prefigured, but there is no sense for what purpose that resurrection would occur.

Where would we all go, and how? I prefer to consider that perhaps this phrase is addressed to we, the living, who must raise ourselves again as we leave the cemetery and make our ways back to your lives.

The Rabbi continued to look down at his prayer book. "Righteous in all his ways, the Rock who is perfect, slow to anger and full of compassion—have compassion, please have pity and spare parents and children, for Yours, O Master, are forgiveness and compassion. You are righteous, Lord, in bringing death and giving life, in your hand is the safekeeping of all spirits. Far be it from You to erase our remembrance. (another translation: it would be *sacrilegious* for You our memory to erase.) May now Your eyes be open toward us in compassion, for Yours, O Master, are compassion and forgiveness." A curious word 'righteous:' one definition of it means 'justified morally,' or 'conforming to the standard of divine or moral law.' But if the law comes from God, then how can God ever be described as righteous? God cannot be righteous because God does not conform to law. God *is* law and death is that law; it must merely be accepted. Again, we are in our prayer justifying the judgment. What we ask is not to be free from death but to be free from our fear of it. We ask that the death of our loved ones not destroy us as well. We must go on. We are all either parents or children, and some of us are both. Death is only the fulfillment of law that living in the world requires; we reside no longer in the Garden. In its perfection, Death has no value of good or bad or right or wrong. Death merely is. But what could possibly justify the deaths of the children in the camps? Nothing, I think, but perhaps it might be said that with that occurrence God had nothing to do.

And even as this prayer asks too simplistically for God to comfort the parents and children of she who lies at the bottom of this grave, so too does it justify God by acknowledging that we are humans requiring forgiveness, mercy and compassion. In our own lives, we have caused so many deaths—we have such need for forgiveness, compassion, and mercy. The Judgment of the Judgment we recite over this grave sends us back hopefully to a better life.

And then, we are condemned to remember. But I wonder what is it that we are supposed to remember. Is it the inevitability of Death that for the most part is wholly out of our control and which we cannot question, or are we to remember the hope of redemption that God who brings death also promises? When I leave this cemetery, I will ritualistically wash my hands and leave death behind me. But I cannot for the life of me manage to forget my knowledge of the absolute existence of death. There is a curious linguistic construction in this prayer. In the first translation, the prayer suggests that it would be beneath God's self to erase our memory. Were we not to remember, God would cease to be God. Memory is what makes us human, and it is also what makes us moral: Remember the Sabbath Day and keep it holy. Remember that you were slaves in Egypt. Remember to care for the widow, the orphan and the stranger in our midst because you were strangers in the land of Egypt and God took you out with an outstretched arm. Without memory, there is no history, and we would not be human without history. Not to remember would make this whole ceremony superfluous and without moral purpose, and therefore, God would be less than God. Ironically, the acceptance of the judgment makes God God.

But in the alternative translation, for God to take away our memory would be for God to commit sacrilege, the crime or sin of stealing or misappropriating what is consecrated to God's service. It seems that were God to erase our memory then God would be sinning against God's self. Since this is not possible, we declare our acceptance of Death and our faith in God. Our memory seems in this prayer to be in the service of protecting the perfectness of God whose judgments are perfect.

The Rabbi continued to intone the Judgment of the Judgment. "If one lives for a year or a thousand years, what does it profit him? He shall be as if he had never been." As I've always suspected, there is nothing beyond Death; Death is truly the end. *As if he had never been shall he be.* But what then of memory? Is it Death we must remember and not the person who has died? If so, then what is all this ceremony about? Are funerals staged to remember Death rather than mourn for the one who has died? Not really, but mourning must end. Rav says, "Only after twelve months does one begin to forget the dead," and yet we pray that we always remember. Rabbi Judah said in the name of Rav, "When a man indulges in excessive grief for his dead, he will so find himself weeping for another dead." The latter death would be that of the excessive mourner. We must leave death and return to life; the dead are gone. It is *that* that we must remember.

Almost in answer to my question, the Rabbi intones: "Blessed is He for his judgment is true, And in His sight He surveys all. He repays everything with His eye, and He recompenses man in accord with his account and just desert. And all must render acknowledgment to his name." God does not cause death, but God does watch it. Our actions have consequences, for God repays everything with his *eye* and not with his hand. That is, our deeds are not hidden, and they have consequences in this world, but our deaths are not a consequence of our lives. Regardless of our lives, we will die, though when that will occur remains unknown to us. Who would know the hour of his death? It is an interesting translation here: in God's sight, God recompenses man in accord with his account and just deserts. I think of Hamlet: "Treat every man according to his own deserts and who should 'scape whipping." Why do the good die young, then? And why did the children die? I cannot answer that, but I do know that everyone must die. It might be a desperate, childish threat implicit in this prayer from which each of us standing here about this grave hopes to be saved. Torah says that compensation must be an eye for an eye and a tooth for a tooth, but the Rabbis are quite clear that this refers only to pecuniary recompense. Thus, it is that the recompense God makes may not be measured by the deaths that mark this cemetery, but rather, must be known outside of it in the world. To each according to his needs and from each according to his ability. If you have built your castles in the air, now you must put the foundations under them. There is meaning in the fall of the sparrow. Sometimes I think there is someone there, at times it's only me. We must all pay greater attention.

This ceremony at the grave is meant to be a comfort for the mourners, but perhaps the lady doth protest too much methinks. Who are we trying to convince that the judgment of death is a good and perfect judgment? The repetition bespeaks our continuing doubt. But to doubt the judgment is to doubt God and that cannot be. The body at the bottom of this hole insists that death is real and absolute and unquestionable. The prayer insists on God's righteousness. "We know that God, righteous is your judgment; You are justified when You speak and faultless when You judge. One cannot have questions about the quality of Your judgment. Righteous are you, God, and fair are your Judgments. O Judge, who is true, who judges with righteousness and truth; blessed is the Judge who is true, for all His judgments are righteous and true." We are to be comforted here because all results from God's will, though Death is yet the sentence. But it is Death's sentence and not God's sentence of Death. Death exists because the world exists and not as a punishment of the world. It could not be that Death is a simplistic effect from a caus. How could we ever equate the death of the evil with the death of the children? It is not the singular death that is the judgment, but Death in general. It is Death that exists outside of Eden and defines our life. We are here to remember Death and in so doing, remember our lives to which we must soon return. On the other hand, perhaps the insistence on the inevitability of Death—of this death—*is* a comfort to the mourners: there is nothing we could have done to have prevented this moment. But what then of free will? Well, there are other deaths I might prevent now. Perhaps best considered at another time and in another place.

Somehow, for warmth or comfort, we have moved closer together; we are a collective now, a community of mourners, as it were. Other than our feet crunching the snow in an attempt to simulate movement and warmth, only the Rabbi's voice is heard. We stare at the great hole in the earth, and we listen. "Great in counsel and mighty in deed, that Your eyes are attentive toward all the ways of mankind, to give each man according to his ways and the fruit of his deeds. To declare that God is just. My rock, there is no wrong in Him." I must say, I hear echoes of Marx here, and I wonder if the rhythm of the Acceptance of the Judgment influenced his mighty phrase, "To each according to his need, from each according to his abilities." Of course, Marx's hope was but a dream, but we too would believe that in this world there is justice not that God exercises but that God oversees. It is we who must enact this justice. God does not require justice, only we humans do, but God requires us to enact it. "Justice, justice, thou shalt pursue." We urge ourselves here to be strong. This ceremony is about us, the living. "The souls of all the living are in your hand, with righteousness are filled Your saving right hand and your chastising left hand. Have mercy on the remnant of the flock of Your hand, and say to the Angel of Death, *Hold back your hand!*" No, I think that it is our hands of which we speak, and standing about this grave, we are, indeed, the remnant of the flock. As we stand here at the open grave, we pray that though death is present, it be not here.

The Rabbi paused, and taking a deep breath, spoke the final lines. "God gave, and God took away; let the Name of God be blessed. He is the Merciful One, is forgiving of iniquity and does not destroy; frequently He withdraws his anger, not arousing His entire wrath." It is a resolution of sorts.

/*leggiero*/ I am thinking of the film, *The Curious Case of Benjamin Button*.

/*mesto*/ Benjamin (the name of Jacob's youngest child, though not his favorite) Button is born looking old, and the course of his life is reversed. As the years progress, he becomes younger. Though born physically old, he is not born with the wisdom of those who have already lived their lives. As with the rest of us, he must learn life by living it, and while backwards, his life runs to the same end, death. It seems to me that what is significant here is that Benjamin's learning is saturated from the beginning by mortality. What Benjamin learns derives from his being out in the world, but all his learning seems founded on the awareness of his mortality, on death and loss.

As with the rest of us, Benjamin carries death within him from birth, but Benjamin Button is born emblematic of that end to which we all will arrive. Not only is he born looking like an old man, but he resides during most of his 'childhood' in an early twentieth century version of an assisted living residence, returning regularly to it from his forays out into the world. And every time Benjamin returns home, someone else in the home has died. Even as Benjamin constantly *appears* younger, the world and he inexorably grow older, and significant pieces of it die. Though Benjamin *appears* old from the beginning of his life, he is born with none of the knowledge that living brings. He must still learn everything by himself. And though Benjamin is apparently surrounded by the wisdom of the elderly, none of that wisdom serves him much purpose. In fact, what wisdom he is offered comes to him mostly as tall tales or piano lessons. It is out in the world permeated as it is by loss, disappointment, destruction and death that Benjamin learns. What he might have learned from the aged remains unavailable to him, and though it is the curious fate of Benjamin Button to age and die, he must do so without any of the familiar signs which might offer him comfort, and he must do so completely alone. For him, everything along the way to dusty death appears different to him than to all of the rest, as if he were walking backwards alongside a brother but towards the same destination. Benjamin Button is forever out of synch with the world, and his brief moments of happiness must be inevitably fleeting. Benjamin can grow old with no one. There can be no comfort in his aging. Benjamin Button moves toward death in the opposite direction from the rest of us, but he moves inexorably towards it. He will die unlearned and ignorant—an infant.

Indeed, in this film, nothing is learned in this world. The film begins with Benjamin's birth at the end of the first great moral breach of the twentieth century, World War I, and it ends with the waters flooding through the broken levee announcing and prefiguring the moral failure of the response to the human devastation wrought by the Hurricane known as Katrina. The floodwaters will soon engulf the curious clock that was made to run backwards even as they will soon cover the city of New Orleans. In the movie, this strange and doomed device was the creation of a Mr. Gateau and was commissioned before World War I to celebrate the newly renovated New Orleans train station. But Gateau made the clock to run backwards, hoping to change the course of history and make time move in reverse and stop the killing and destruction of the War in which his own son had recently been lost. Alas, the clock ran backwards but time moved intractably forward. Making time run backwards certainly could not halt death, and it certainly could not stop the regular destructions and devastations that human stupidity and callousness produced in the world. Benjamin Button's life, too, runs in reverse, but there is no escaping life's losses or inevitable death.

/*grazioso*/ There is death and loss everywhere Benjamin goes; indeed, he carries mortality, as do the rest of us, as part of his being. And it crosses my mind now that what is curious, perhaps, about the case of Benjamin Button, is that there is nothing curious about it at all: he is just like us. Forever out of synch, alienated, and fatally mortal, trying to make his way in a world in which too much of that death and destruction derives from moral failure rather than natural causes, Benjamin's joys are as contingent and ephemeral as are those of our own lives, framed as they are forever by death.

/*mesto*/ The Rabbi was an older man well into his 70s. He wore a long dark brown cloth coat, and around his neck he had wrapped a black scarf. He had finished reading from his prayer book and looked around at the mourners gathered about the gravesite. He was standing at the foot of it, and before him, the earth gaped open. Two piles of dirt lay high on either side, and unsteadily amidst the mounds stood the gathered mourners on the uneven ground. It seemed that there was too much dirt necessary to bury this child. Not four months ago, this boy had led the congregation in Shabbat prayer, had been called to the Torah for the first time as an adult member of the community, and had instructed the congregation about some of the things that he had learned while he studied and prepared for that event. His body lay now in this plain pine box. At the Rabbi's feet was a marker, placed there by the cemetery to note the location of Jonathan's grave. It was a small blue plaque with just his name. To note the dates of his life would have been too cruel. This marker would remain here in the earth until a more permanent gravestone would be erected, probably in a year hence. Jonathan was to be buried in the grave site purchased originally for his parents. Unnaturally, the parents would eventually follow their son here. To the right and left and behind this site were gravestones, and along the top, stones of various shapes and sizes had been set in an irregular row. Someone had been here.

The cemetery consisted of hundreds of acres, and occupied several square miles of passive land. We stood at one end of the site, but I felt as if no matter where we stood, we stood at the center of the cemetery. Amidst all of this quiet, amidst all of the death, we yet breathed, we moved, we mourned. The Rabbi placed his prayer book into the large pockets of his coat and placed his arms down again by his side. He said, "We do our duty to the dead by burying them ourselves," and he pulled out one of the three shovels that had been embedded like spikes in the piles of dirt. "When you have finished, place the shovel back into the dirt where the next person wishing to help bury our friend will find it; we don't want to hand the shovel off in order to show that this is not a task we are anxious to complete." He continued, "You might dig first using the back of the shovel, also because this is a task that we would prefer not to do and are not in a hurry to complete." Then, turning the shovel about so that its rounded bottom faced up, he forcefully pushed it into the mound. As he lifted the shovel out, the dirt slipped quickly off of the shovel's sides and back onto the mound, but the Rabbi swung the shovel over the foot of the grave and a few remaining grains of dirt floated down into the open hole. Then, the Rabbi turned the shovel about, and with some vigor he drove the face into the mound of dirt to his right. Lifting the full shovel, he dropped the dirt into the grave in which now only the coffin lay at rest. This was not a feathery dropping, and the dirt made not a hollow sound but rather an empty one when it hit the filled wooden box. The Rabbi continued in this fashion to shovel dirt into the grave, and each time the dirt fell, the sound within the grave deepened and carried less resonance. Though the day was cold, small beads of perspiration had begun to appear on the Rabbi's brow and his breathing had grown more rapid and shallow with his effort. Soon, he stuck the shovel back into the mound and stepped back from the gravesite. For a moment, no one moved, and then hands reached toward the shovel he had returned to the dirt, and on the other side of the site, hands reached for the other two shovels stuck in the mounds, and the work of burying the child began in earnest. Most worked for thirty or forty seconds, as if to engage longer was to show too much willingness to bury, but the participation was steady. No one but the numbed parents and sister did not aid in burying Jonathan Rothstein. Not a word was spoken, and as the wooden coffin disappeared under the piles of dirt, the sound of the falling dirt continued to lessen. After twenty minutes, the earth was covered whole again. There were no mounds in which to spear the shovels and so they remained in the hands of the last to use them.

The Rabbi spoke, and everyone spoke with him, *"Yis-ga-dal ve'yit ka-dash sh'mei ra-ba:" it was the familiar* words of the Mourner's Kaddish. "Exalted and hallowed be God's greatness/ In this world of Your creation. May your will be fulfilled, And your sovereignty revealed, And the life of the whole house of Israel speedily and soon. And say, Amen." Here again not a mention of the deceased, not even a mention of death. In this prayer recited by the mourners before the grave of this child, the reference was to a life fulfilling God's work—to care for the widow, the orphan, and the stranger in our midst. God's will is justice.

The Kaddish continued, "May You be blessed forever, Even to all eternity. May You most Holy One, be blessed, Praised and honored, extolled and glorified, Adored and exalted above all else. Blessed are You. Beyond all blessings and hymns, praises and consolations That may be uttered in this world, In the days of our lifetime, And say, Amen." It is this life with which we are concerned, the days of our lifetime, and as we stand about this grave into which we have placed Jonathan Rothstein, our Kaddish reminds us that it is life we must celebrate.

God, who is beyond all blessings of praise *and* consolations, is blessed? No, I think this mourner's prayer is directed at us the mourners. We remind ourselves here that we are everything and that we are nothing. We aspire to achieve, but we will not fully attain all that we desire *in the days of our lifetime.* And then at that time of our deaths, we will not utter the words any more, though others may utter them. And that is the way life and death should be, I think. "May peace abundant descend from heaven/With life for us and for all Israel, And say, Amen." I think of Yeats' cabin, of clay and wattles made, built on the Lake Isle of Innisfree where peace comes dropping slow. Not softly, but slow. The peace here consists of our lives in which we work for the peace that must exist amongst us. It is us God needs for this work, for without our work there can be no peace.

/*affetuoso*/ "May God, Who makes peace on high, Bring peace to all and to all Israel." Interesting that the Kaddish does not ask that God make peace here on earth as God does in Heaven. I suppose that such is a human task. I am glad for that, I think. "May God, Who makes peace on high, Bring peace to all and to all Israel."

And let us say, Amen.

THIRD MOVEMENT
Scherzo

|scherzando| *"Oh, no. You can't fool me. There ain't no Sanity Clause."*

This following is a joke. Really.

A story is told: In a small town in the Ukraine at the turn of the century before last, a rumor quickly spread that a young Christian girl had been found dead along the side of road. She had been murdered! The slander of blood libel hung in the air like the smoke that would spew from the chimneys at Auschwitz, and the Jews of this small town understood immediately the vicious consequences this event would have on them. There would be rioting, looting and murderous attacks on the Jewish community. There would occur another pogrom from which who could know who would survive. News of the calamity spread like an arson fire (a cruel simile here, but perhaps an appropriate one), as neighbor ran to neighbor spreading what she had heard, weeping and wailing over the inevitable and horrible consequences. As if by instinct, the Jews all gathered in their *shul* where the Rabbi would surely know what would have to be done to prepare for what all knew would soon occur. The old and wizened Rabbi stood before his congregation and raised his hands, and the people ceased their troubled talk. "My dear friends," he began. "God's ways are mysterious, but we must . . . " Suddenly, before the Rabbi spoke another syllable, the door of the shul slammed open and a breathless messenger, as if he were Pheidippides and had run from Marathon to Athens to announce the victory of the Greeks over the Persians, made his way to the Rabbi and in triumphant exhaustion, fell at his feet. "I have news, good news, good news," he gasped. The people all edged closer to hear of their redemption. "The child who was murdered, the young girl, she was Jewish!!"

This joke is not really very funny, but it is a joke nonetheless. I know that because I read it in a book dedicated to jokes. Its humor, horrible though it may be, speaks of a world in which such absurd logic makes sense. Within the nonsense of the joke, there is sense; the nonsense in the joke depends upon the existence of an absurdity outside of the joke, though in this case, the absurdity is tragic. It says: How fortunate that the girl murdered was Jewish, for though the child met with a violent end, the community itself would be spared violence!! All that mattered now was that the murdered girl was Jewish and therefore, for the hate-filled community of anti-Semites, blood libel would not be the motive, and the pogrom—that would ultimately occur in its time—at least would not happen *now*. And this perverse logic brings to the terrified Jews great relief!

This joke speaks to lives lived in a world governed by such madness. What occurs in the joke approaches too close to reality, and though the events narrated make no sense other than a tragic one, out of our anguish we create humor or we will succumb to the hopelessness and despair upon which this joke rests and against which it protests. Jokes offer the illusion of a power that is denied us in this world.

A story is told: Two Jews were walking down a street in pre-World War II Berlin when suddenly they notice that they are being followed by those who might be referred to as two young hooligans. The night was dark and the Jews were far from home. "Sigmund," says one to his companion, "we better get out of here. There are two of them and we're alone!" Acknowledging the terrifying helplessness of the Jews in Nazi Germany, this joke also protests against it.

Jokes serve crucial psychical purpose. At their best, they protect us from going insane, though at their worst, they can promote a murderous madness. Freud attributes the effectiveness of jokes to their "ability to provide pleasure against the objections raised by criticism that would put an end to pleasure." In this sense, jokes permit us to enjoy those things our superegos have declared it wrong (or too dangerous) to enjoy. Sex, drugs and rock n' roll, to speak metaphorically.

A story is told: An older couple was sitting in front of their television one night watching *Desperate Housewives*. It must have been (for them!) a particularly prurient episode, and perhaps it called up some interesting romantic memories. The woman turned to her husband and put her hand lovingly on his. "Dear, have *we* ever had mutual orgasm?"

Without taking his eyes from the television screen he answered,

"No, we've always had Allstate."

Jokes defend us against our fears and allow us to pass judgment on our enemies (real or illusory) when we would normally be afraid to do so.

A story is told: Reuven is a good man, and he has worked hard all of his life. He arose early—almost always up before the sun—ate his breakfast alone, prepared his meager lunch and thermos of hot coffee, and quietly left his house awakening no one. He took the subway downtown, crowded into the car so tightly that he couldn't even open his newspaper, and then walked to his office. He sat down in his cubicle, turned on the computer and began work. Every morning, he shuffled papers, placing them sometimes on the right side of his desk and sometimes on the left side, before typing something. His colleague, Chaim, who performed the same work, leaned over the wall and said, "Coffee break!" Either Chaim came to Reuven's office and sat down in the chair that rested in the corner of the cubicle, or Reuven joined Chaim in his cubicle sitting in the identically styled chair in the corner of Chaim's area. Each would pour his coffee from his thermos into a cheap ceramic mug and for fifteen minutes engage in very small talk. At lunch, the two often dined at the rear of the office in the small break room cluttered with half-filled coffee cups, plastic sandwich wrappers and emptied soda bottles, and blanketed with the smell of food. In summer, Chaim and Reuven sometimes lunched on a bench under a tree in front of the office building. They sat outside as if they had only recently discovered its existence.

Once, Reuven was sitting on the toilet and in the stall right next to him—just like in his office cubicle—was his friend, Chaim. "Chaim," he called through the walls and sighed, "is this considered work or pleasure?"

For a moment it was quiet, and then Chaim said, "I think it is definitely pleasure, because if it were work the boss would ask me to do this for him." At their best, jokes protest against oppression, prejudice and hate, and at their worst, alas, they can perpetuate such practices.

I consider that jokes serve as a form of protest against the world that, justly or unjustly, denies pleasure. We rail against the world that abuses us physically or psychically with its power. We protest with our jokes against our feelings of powerlessness. For me, the Marx Brothers are the quintessential exemplar of this kind of joke. With their nonsense, they puncture all pretense to sense, and our pleasure in their antics derives in large part from their refusal to adhere to any logic by which we are irrevocably bound in this life!! The world of the Marx Brothers is characterized by chaos and is not intended to make sense, thank goodness, and it debunks the world that functions, alas, with insufferable logic and control. "Why would I join any club that would have me as a member?" Groucho Marx wonders. In *Horsefeathers*, Groucho, assuming the role of Quincy Adams Wagstaff, the newly appointed President of Huxley College, begins his address at the opening academic convocation, like many I have been invited to attend over the past forty years. "Members of the faculty, faculty members, students of Huxley, and Huxley students. I guess that covers everything." Groucho as Wagstaff continues: "Well, I thought my razor was dull until I heard this speech, and that reminds me of a story that's so dirty I'm ashamed to think of it myself." Wagstaff, unflappable, proceeds with his opening address, but he never makes more sense. I wonder how many such speeches—convocational or otherwise—do make sense? Indeed, a colleague once remarked that at the beginning of a new school year each September he felt eager and restless to burst out of the starting gate, as it were, and I remarked that I experienced a similar anticipation, but before they (the ubiquitous *they*) open the gate and let the race begin, they first make you stand *behind* the horse.

Jokes argue for utopia as a protest by those without power against the ways the world exercises such power.

A story is told: After the Anschluss, a Jew sought to leave Austria, and so he went to a travel agent to study his options. The travel agent, a lovely and sympathetic woman, pulled out a large globe and began to describe the immigration requirements for various 'safe' countries. In one country, a labor permit was necessary, but the man did not possess one; in another country only immigrants with a certain amount of liquid capital were admitted. Alas, the man possessed little means. In yet another, the Austrian passport was no longer recognized; in a fourth, immigration had been severely restricted; and in a fifth, Jews were forbidden entrance altogether. "Oy vey," sighed the Jew, resting his hand on his cheek and looking imploringly at the travel agent, "Maybe you have another globe?" Jokes offer us an alternative world where we may assume our proper stature and power. Jokes permit us to say out loud what we would normally be afraid to express—sometimes, as in the case of ethnic, racist or sexist jokes, with much good reason. Telling jokes—and laughing when they are heard—gives us back what we believe the world has already taken. Freud says that 'tendentious jokes,' those that express an opinion, are "useful in order to make aggressiveness or criticism possible against persons in exalted positions who claim to exercise authority." Again, the quintessential comics are the Marx Brothers in whose films all pomposity and authority is deflated. A tendentious joke—and the Marx Brothers made whole movies filled with them—is rebellion against authority. In a Marx Brothers movie, no power is left standing.

It seems to me that the more I look for order and rationality in the world, the more humorous the world seems to me and the more I laugh. If I want the world to make sense, I can only do so by telling jokes about it. An ironic sense is a combative stance against the world's absurdity. Without jokes we would be without hope. Indeed, Freud speculates that the greater our sense of joy the less we have need for jokes. He writes, "It is most instructive to observe how the standards of joking sink as spirits rise." I must admit that in these times I have a great need of jokes. Just look at any newspaper any day, anytime, anywhere. Even in Torah, the absurd takes its stand against unconstrained power, human arrogance, stupidity and greed. Authority is undermined, and humor results. In the story of Balaam and Balak and the movies of the Marx Brothers, I find a template for not a few contemporary jokes. Now, one could argue that in Scripture such debunking serves some higher moral and spiritual purpose, but who is to say that the Groucho, Chico and Harpo do not mean to offer us strategies for how to live better in this world. Humor is certainly a primary strategy. In both the story of Balaam and Balak and in the adventures of the Marx brothers, human conceit and power are mocked and rendered ineffective.

A story is told: Balak, King of Moab, had weighty concerns regarding the growing strength of the wandering Israelites who recently had secured a significant military victory against Sihon, King of the Amorites. As Balak understood the story narrated to him, the Israelites had first suffered a cruel military defeat at the hands of the Amalekites, Israel's historical enemy and the paradigmatic anti-Semite. This defeat denied the Israelites entrance to the land of Canaan from the South, and so Moses turned the wandering people towards the North and requested that King Sihon allow the Israelites to pass through the Amorite land on their way to Canaan. Moses offered Sihon a guarantee that in their passage through the land the wandering people would not veer off the path or venture into Amorite fields or vineyards, and certainly they would not drink from the wells. But Sihon refused the Israelites request, and instead, assuming the people to be weak, gathered together his army and attacked, thinking to decimate this wandering, irksome community. Sihon failed miserably. As Torah succinctly reports, "But Israel put them to the sword and took possession of their land." So there! Defeating Sihon gave Israel access to lands the Sihonites had already won from the Moabites, and the wandering Israelite people moved closer to their desire to enter the land—this time from the West—that had been promised them. Following this victory over the Amorites, the Israelites marched on to Bashan, and when King Og came out to do battle with them, the Israelites defeated him handily as well and took possession of that country. Reading Torah, I sometimes feel that I am reading *The New York Times* or *Ha-aretz.*

Anyway, these reported military victories upset Balak through whose land the Israelites had next to pass en route to the Promised Land. I suspect the newspapers were replete with reports of the Israelites' successes, and filled with dire editorial foreboding predicting national tragedy unless something were soon done to stop the trespassing Israelite forces. I suspect they blamed the teachers and the educational system for the current state of national affairs. Security had probably been set at level red. Balak said to his advisors, "Now this congregation will lick clean all that is about us as an ox licks up the grass of the field," voicing serious misgivings about the capacity of his army to defeat what should have been a rag-tag people. Seemingly desperate and frightfully concerned with the possibility of mass destruction, Balak turned to the supernatural for aid and succor. This type of appeal had been made before.

A story is told: When the Russians invaded Czechoslovakia in 1968, the citizenry was plunged into fear and despair. Alexander Dubček, Czechoslovakia's president was sorely troubled, and had no plan or strategy to relieve his beloved country from the Russian tyranny. His cabinet had fled into hiding, his secret service guard had defected to the Russian side, his phone lines had been tapped, and he strongly suspected that he was being watched at every minute by the Secret Police. Despondent, Dubček turned to a well-known Jewish soothsayer, a direct descendant of Rabbi Judah Lowe, himself famous for having created in the 16th century the mythical Golem designed to protect the Jewish citizens of Prague from anti-Semitic attacks. The soothsayer smiled warmly and told Dubček that he need not fret;

there was yet hope for Czechoslovakia, and that for the near future two viable possibilities existed, one natural and one supernatural."

"Tell me both," said Dubček desperately.

"Well," the soothsayer began, "the natural one is that the archangel Michael will come down wielding a fiery sword and chase out the invading Russians, return the country to independence and restore you to your rightful place."

"And what is the supernatural possibility?" Dubček asked dubiously.

"Well," said the soothsayer, stroking his grey beard, "the supernatural possibility is that the Russians will leave all by themselves."

Finally, there was no hope for Czechoslovakia.

And so Balak sent word to Balaam, son of Beor, requesting his aid in dealing with the Israelites. Apparently, Balaam had acquired a considerable reputation as a sorcerer and even perhaps a prophet, and Balak appealed to Balaam to put a curse upon the Israelite people to ensure Balak's victory over them and drive them out of his land. "For I know that he whom you bless is blessed indeed, and he whom you curse is cursed." All the power rested in Balaam. Balak may not have known or had not fully considered that the Israelites had been aided all along—well, at least for so long as they did not complain or rebel—by some supernatural support. They were not going to leave Balak's land voluntarily. They were already wanderers; where would they go?

But Balaam was no fool, and he possessed important information not available to Balak. Balaam had acquired some strategical knowledge of the Israelite God, and so before he acceded to Balak's request, he sought out and then awaited some word from the Israelite God about the viability of such a mission. Balaam, not an unwise man, intended to accept the best offer. God told Balaam not to curse the Israelites "for they are blessed." Of course, the recent plagues and hardships that God had visited upon this rebellious and petulant people might have suggested otherwise. (Tevye says, "He's supposed to be our merciful Father; well, He's had such mercy on me that I hope I've seen the last of it—and He better not charge me extra for saying that.") But lately, despite the larger problem of the seemingly endless wandering , the Israelite people had realized some success in their military efforts and appeared to be a formidable enemy. The people were moving relentlessly toward the Promised Land. And so

Balaam took heed of God's proscription and sent word to Balak that, despite the offer, he would not agree to journey to Moab to curse the Israelites.

But Balak, like Groucho in his endless and fruitless pursuit of Margaret DuMont, was not so easily put off. Unlike Groucho, Balak had every expectation of getting what he wanted. Balak must have been very worried about the military potency of the Israelite people; he sent a second time to Balaam for succor, but this time with a far more generous offer—one, perhaps, that he suspected Balaam could not refuse. Balak offered him great riches. To paraphrase Tevye again, if only Balak had listened to what the Bible says, he would never have believed in False Profits. Balaam again cautiously waited for word from God, and this time, God surprisingly agreed to let him go, though God demanded that when Balaam spoke, he must say only those words that God would place in his mouth. Balaam agreed. If only Balaam had listened to what the Bible says, he would never have believed in False Profits. I suspect that Balaam was thinking only of the money he would earn, or perhaps he did not think God would deceive him and that he had, indeed, received God's leave to attend Balak. Balaam headed out with the Moabite emissaries sent to transport him to their land!

Now it is still unclear to me from the story what exactly next occurred, but apparently sometime between when God gave qualified permission for Balaam to travel to Balak and the start of the journey, God became incensed at Balaam's going. An angel came to stand before the expedition and blocked the path forward. The angel, however, was visible only to Balaam's donkey, which, upon seeing the angel, swerved out of the road and into the fields so as not to run into it. Whether the donkey knew that this was God's angel, the Torah does not say, but given what occurs next, I would argue that this was a very prescient donkey. As I've said, Balaam did not see the angel and thought that the donkey was merely being stubborn and oppositional. Balaam, not one to be defied (hence perhaps his willingness to attend Balak) beat the donkey and steered it (unwillingly, I suspect) back onto the road where the travelers continued on.

I'm remembering the scenes in *Duck Soup* when Rufus Firefly (Groucho), newly appointed leader of Fredonia, hires Harpo to transport him about town. Climbing into the sidecar of Harpo's motorbike, Firefly declares authoritatively, "I've got an appointment to insult Ambassador Trentino and I don't want to keep him waiting. Step on it." Harpo crouches down in his seat behind the handlebars, focuses intently on the road ahead, and zooms off on the motorbike, leaving behind the sidecar with Firefly in it. Firefly watches the motorbike disappear, and sitting atop the sidecar, his fist underneath his chin, says with some concern but more resignation, "This is the fifth trip I've made today and I haven't been anywhere yet." Not the willful donkey but a similar absurdity blocks Firefly's way.

Balaam does not have the equanimity and forbearance that Firefly displays. He already feels seriously constrained by a God to whom he offers respect but not obeisance. He would get to his assignation as quickly and as comfortably and as nobly as possible. But the angel continued to frustrate Balaam's journey, placing itself again before the donkey. This time, the expedition was traveling through vineyards on a narrow path that seems to have been bounded on both sides by a stone fence. The donkey tried to avoid the angel that only it could see, and veered first to the right and then to the left, each time squeezing Balaam's foot against the stonewall causing him considerable physical discomfort. In pain, anger and frustration, Balaam beat the donkey mercilessly. Unable to move in any direction, the poor donkey just lay down in place. But this did not abate Balaam's fury, and he continued his violent assault on the hapless animal. "You have made a mockery of me," Balaam swore at the donkey, thinking of his own reputation. Perhaps it was what he had always primarily considered. The aggrandizement of his reputation might have led him to agree to accompany Balak's messengers in the first place:. He was flattered by the request, though he must have suspected that no good was going to come of his mission.

Interestingly, the schemes of Groucho's movie characters, always dubious and haphazardly elaborated, are never realized when they are motivated by self-aggrandizement. His characters are forever attempting to partner with a rich dowager and attain a life style to which he would like to become accustomed. Wooing Mrs. Potter in Cocoanuts, he offers this romantic scenario: "What I meant was, if we had a nice little bungalow and you was on the inside and I was on the outside trying to get in, and me inside trying to get out or, no you're inside out and I was upside—I'll tell you, if you don't hear from me by next Friday, the whole thing's off." In Duck Soup, Firefly, learning that Mrs. Teasdale's rich husband is deceased, proposes to her, "Will you marry me? Did he leave you any money? Answer the second question first." When she admits that she has inherited his fortune, Firefly says, "Is that so? Can't you see what I'm trying to tell you? I love you." Put money in thy purse! In fact, Groucho never gets the girl, though it be the rich Margaret DuMont or the beautiful blondes he tries to seduce throughout the films. In fact, only when

Groucho and his brothers scheme to help others (as in *A Day at the Races* or *A Night at the Opera*) does Groucho realize some degree of success. There is in the end, a strong moral sense in the Marx Brothers' movies. Though violence is always threatened, it is never real. *"I've a good mind to join a club and beat you over the head with it,"* Groucho declares at a forever nonplussed adversary personified in Chico.

And though Groucho is forever scheming, he never seems surprised that his plans do not work out as he would have hoped. Of course, Groucho's plans are as ill-conceived as are those of Balaam and Balak. Groucho is always trying to fool someone out of her/his money, or pretending to a position of authority for which he has no claim, or assuming a knowledge he does not possess. In *A Night at the Opera,* he first pretends to serve as a professional mediator for Mrs. Claypool's entrance into society, and then he passes himself off as a skillful agent for an opera company. In *A Day at the Races,* Groucho poses as a medical doctor, and in *Horsefeathers* as a college president. For each role, he is thoroughly unsuited and only chaos results from his complete lack of competence! But though Groucho may not be smart, he is clever. As one option closes inevitably down, he simply develops another scheme until the world—often represented by Chico and Harpo—ultimately foils all his plans. In *Duck Soup,* Groucho, once more seeking transportation, approaches Harpo waiting in the motorcycle and side car. "Oh, no, you don't," he says to Harpo in the driver's seat. "I'm not taking any more chances. You can only fool a Firefly twice. This time *you* ride in the sidecar." Crouching down behind the handlebars and focused intently ahead, Groucho prepares to ride out when the sidecar in which Harpo sits takes off leaving the motorcycle behind. Groucho always plots to succeed, but is never surprised or daunted by his failures. Unmoving and unmovable, he sits on the motorcycle with his hand on his cheek and says, "This is the only way to travel."

Balaam had no similar equanimity or resourcefulness. When his plans were frustrated, he responded with aggression and displeasure. Balaam began to beat the donkey mercilessly. Finally, the beleaguered animal looked imploringly up at Balaam and unlike Raskolnikov's mute and suffering horse, objected: "I am the ass that you have been riding all along until this day. Have I ever been in the habit of doing thus to you." There is no report in Torah of Balaam's reaction to the talking ass—years before Ed, the talking horse—but I would have to believe that he suffered a bit of shock. It is not every day that a domestic animal complains about its present state in language that we would understand.

A story is told: In a rather fashionable area of New York City a Frenchman walks into a bar with a parrot on his shoulder. On the parrot's head is a New York Yankee baseball cap. "Hey, that's adorable," the bartender said, "where'd you get that?"

And the parrot said, "In France. They've got millions of them there."

I am almost certain that Balaam did not find the incident of the talking donkey at all humorous. Balaam does not apologize or excuse his vicious behavior. I cannot help but see some humor in the image I hold of the donkey's actions. Following the Torah's account of harrowing events at Sinai and the wanderings in the desert, subsequent to the miraculous appearances of food and water in the midst of the waste of the desert; following the series of serious internal rebellions and the resultant calamities that followed from them; and coming on the heels of several successful and unsuccessful military engagements, this scene of a talking donkey stubbornly refusing to giddy to Balaam's -ap and then protesting to the somewhat contrite Balaam of the injustice done it, possesses not enough gravity and too much levity to be taken seriously. There is not often humor in the Bible, (some would claim there is none at all!) but at shul this week I found myself chortling liberally and just a bit too loudly at this story of Balaam and Balak. Here, the King's sorcerer and prophet on a mission of national interest and personal benefit was berated by a donkey, a scene of slapstick and farce to match that in any Marx Brothers movie.

At the opening of *A Day at the Races*, Dr. Hackenbush, his stethoscope pressed against the horse's chest, exhorts the horse. "Inhale, exhale, inhale, exhale," Suddenly, Hackenbush receives a telegram calling him from his animal practice to assume the position as head doctor at an expensive sanitarium where he will specifically treat (and care for) the wealthy Mrs. Upjohn whose opinion of Hackenbush far exceeds his capabilities. "Well," she says, "I never knew there was so much wrong with me until I started going to Dr Hackenbush."

Upon receipt of the invitation, Hackenbush immediately dons his coat and heads for the exit door, but his arm gets stuck in the sleeve in which a puppy is fast asleep. He removes it lovingly and hands it over to the messenger, before hurrying once more toward the exit. But he is called back by the whinny of the horse he had been examining. Hackenbush reaches into his pocket and pulls out a huge round pill that he offers to the horse as he would offer it a sugar cube. "Take one of those every half-mile and call me if there is any change!"

Both Hackenbush and Balaam are controlled by their animals, but Balaam displays no feeling for his donkey. Though Balaam and Hackenbush seem to be in the game for the money, Hackenbush never responds to obstructions with impatience or anger. The world consistently frustrates Groucho's purposes, absurd though they may appear, but Groucho *expects* to be treated so in the world, and he remains remarkably resilient to frustration. When one avenue closes, he facilely moves onto the next with an equally absurd contingent plan. His frustrations are personal but never serious. In *Monkey Business*, Groucho confronts the captain of the cruise ship: "I want to register a complaint. Do you know who sneaked into my stateroom at three o'clock this morning? Nobody, and that's my complaint. I want gaiety, laughter, ha-cha-cha. Another thing, I don't care for the way you're running this boat. Why don't you get in the back seat for a while and let your wife drive." *Oh, no. You can't fool me. There ain't no Sanity Clause.*

Torah continues: "Then the Lord uncovered Balaam's eyes, and he saw the angel of the Lord standing in the way, his drawn sword in his hand." Awed, though also, I think, cowed, Balaam bowed to the ground. The angel berated Balaam and announced that if the donkey had not shied away from the angel three times, the angel would have slain Balaam with his sword "for the errand is obnoxious to me." This must certainly be news to Balaam who thought he had been given leave to attend to Balak. Now terrified and humbled, Balaam offers to forgo the mission. However, the angel orders him to continue on the journey and conveys this caveat: "But you must say nothing except what I tell you." First, the donkey and now, the angel have thwarted Balaam's purposes. I imagine he proceeded on to his meeting with Balak without much enthusiasm. I suspect his interest in the mission had vanished, and his expectations for success considerably diminished.

In *Cocoanuts*, Groucho plays Mr. Hammer, a hotel owner and real estate entrepreneur trying to sell land in Florida. To the hotel come Chico and Harpo, drawn by newspaper advertisements suggesting "Big boom in Florida." Declaring themselves a "coupla big booms," Chico requests a room for himself and his companion. Hammer agrees, but cautions, "I'm not going to have that red-headed fellow running around the lobby. If you want to keep him up in the room, you'll have to catch him in a trap."

"You can't catch him," Chico declares.

"Who is he?" says Hammer.

"He's my partner, but he no speak."

"Oh," says Hammer, "that's your silent partner." Though Harpo may be silent, Hammer knows he will be neither invisible nor without consequence.

In the Biblical story, the angel was Balaam's silent partner and though silent and invisible, would not be without consequence.

Balaam finally arrived at Balak's place of encampment, and I suspect, immediately attempted to excuse his lateness. I don't imagine he accounted for his tardiness by narrating the incident of the talking donkey and the angel. Balaam had his reputation to protect, and he had been summoned exactly for his ability to control events. I am certain that Balaam produced for Balak an excellent story.

Now, Groucho, too, sometimes arrives late in his movies, though he is not prone to admit it. In *A Night at the Opera*, Driftwood is an hour late to his dinner appointment with Mrs. Claypool. She reprimands him: "Mr. Driftwood, you invited me to dine with you at seven o'clock. It is now eight o'clock, and no dinner."

He looks at her without much surprise but not without affront: "What do you mean, no dinner? I just had one of the biggest meals I ever ate in my life, and no thanks to you either." Driftwood has all the while been dining at the next table with a beautiful blonde to whom he hands the check, ("Nine dollars forty cents! This is an outrage. If I were you, I wouldn't pay it!)," and turns immediately to sit down with Mrs. Claypool at her table. And when Mrs. Claypool complains again that she has been waiting an hour for him, Driftwood says, "Yes, with your back to me. When I invite a woman to dinner, I expect her to look at my face. That's the price she has to pay." Driftwood knows his place, but that does not deter him.

Balaam had no such modesty. Taken out on a cliff overlooking a group of the Israelite people whom he is to curse, Balaam told Balak to build him seven altars on which Balaam sacrificed seven bulls and seven rams. And then Balaam removes himself to await some manifestation from God that Balaam will share with Balak. He was now, as per his earlier agreement with God, God's voluble but silent partner. I doubt Balaam shared this piece of news with his employer.

With Balak and his officers standing behind him, Balaam cursed the Israelites. However, all that came out of his mouth was a blessing. Paid to curse the enemy, Balaam was constrained to bless them!

Balak, as might be expected, was appropriately incensed. I imagine him smacking his forehead with the palm of his hand and volubly berating Balaam, even perhaps as Balaam had cast calumny on his donkey. Balak bellowed, "What have you done to me? Here I have brought you to damn my enemies, and instead you have blessed them!"

Balaam looked up sheepishly and somewhat embarrassed, shrugged his shoulders and to himself complained, "I knew this was going to be trouble."

Alarmed by Hammer's wooing, Mrs. Potter says to him, "What in the world is the matter withyou? And he responds, "Oh, I'm not myself tonight. I don't know who I am. One false move and I'm yours. I love you."

Warily she says, "I don't think you'd love me if I were poor," and Hammer responds, "I might, but I'd keep my mouth shut!" Balaam can't do the same!

Balak, hoping a move to a new perspective on the assembled Israelites will improve chances for Balaam's success, moved the entire following to a new location, and once again Balaam commanded him to build seven altars on which to sacrifice seven bulls and seven rams. Again, Balaam went off to seek a manifestation from God, and received the same Heavenly orders. Once again, the curse Balaam intended to speak became a blessing.

Exasperated, Balak complained that it would be better if Balaam should just said nothing: "Don't curse them and don't bless them." Just keep your mouth shut!!! But this despairing request occurred too late.

Balaam, unlike Groucho, did not easily accept defeat or blame. He told Balak, "But I told you [this would happen]: Whatever the Lord says, that I must do!" Balak, frustrated but desperate, offered Balaam one more try, and despite Balaam's ominous premonitions, the company moved to a third location, build once again the seven altars and sacrificed the seven bulls and seven rams upon them. This group had singular purpose and no flexibility; they demanded the world adhere to their purposes. Once again, though Balaam intended to curse the Israelites and collect his reward, he ended up blessing them. Hearing Balaam's words, Balak smacked his hands together—a Biblical version of slapping his forehead—fired Balaam and sent him packing. "Then Balaam set out on his journey back home; and Balak also went his way." *I've a good mind to join a club and beat you over the head with it.*

In the auction scene in *Cocoanuts* when Groucho hires Chico to up the bidding on land parcels: "Now, remember, when the auction starts, if anybody says 100 dollars—"

"I-a say-a 200 dollars—"

"That's grand. Now, if somebody says 200—"

"I-a say 300."

All elements of the plot seem in place. But as soon as the auction begins, the scheme goes awry—Groucho asks for a starting bid of 100 dollars and Chico bids 100 dollars, but when Groucho asks who will bid 200 dollars, Chico bids it. In no time, Chico, who, of course, has no money, bids the parcel up to 600 dollars. "Wrap up that lot and put some poison ivy on it . . ." Groucho orders. With his hand on his cheek he sighs, "Well, I came out even on that one. That was a great success. Yeah, one more success like that and I'll sell my body to a medical institute." Not much improves in the sale of the next lot. Bidding himself up a hundred dollars at a time, Chico foils Groucho's plans. "Well, the auction is practically over. Yes, it's all over but the shooting. I'll attend to that later." Finally, Groucho receives an opening bid of 100 dollars from another bidder, and when Chico ups the bid to 200 dollars, Groucho sells the land to the first and lower bidder. "Believe me, you have to get up early if you want to get out of bed." What did he say?

> "Hey, wait—wait!. What does this say here? This thing here?"
>
> "Oh, that? Oh, that's just the usual clause. That's in every contract. That just says-uh, it says-uh, if any of the parties participating in this contract is shown not to be in their right mind, the entire agreement is automatically nullified."
>
> "Well, I don't know."
>
> "Its alright. That's-that's in every contract. That's—that's what they call a sanity clause.
>
> "Oh, no. You can't fool me. There ain't no Sanity Clause."

Well, yes, the world *is* absurd. There ain't no sanity clause. When, we feel despondent and without hope, perhaps what saves us is our jokes, feeble though they sometimes be.

A story is told: Sven and Ole are out hunting one autumn day. The air is crisp and clean as only a late fall day can be just after Indian summer and right before the cruel advent of a Midwestern winter. But on the day of their manly outing (though you should not imagine great preparations have been undertaken to prepare for this excursion) the heavens are shining a brilliant sky-blue, and the trees blossoming in brilliant shades of reds and oranges and browns. How beautiful Nature seems in its death throes, as Sven and Ole, or Ole and Sven, depending on who takes the lead, wander about seeking to bring home the venison, as the saying goes.

Now, both Sven and Ole have taken the day off to enjoy the weather, the company of their friendship, and the anticipation of the taste of venison for the winter months. From what labor they have taken the day is a fact in question: certainly, they haven't really taken the day off from work, because neither of them is at present gainfully employed, though every morning at nine o'clock they leave the house, appearing industrious even in their lethargy, and head downtown arm-in-arm to the Unemployment Office. It is also true that Lena and Olga, their wives, would not have left Sven and Ole sitting about at home to watch television and drink beer while the women went off to their factory work to earn the income that actually supports the households.

Neither Ole nor Sven has actually shot at anything yet, though they have certainly enjoyed a lovely, restful day thus far. As good friends will do, they discuss their health, including the aches in their knee joints that keep them from heavy lifting, and the regularity of their bowel movements that keep them content. They complain about their wives and the infrequency with which they desire sex, and they may mention some world event they heard rumor of as they stood in line at the unemployment office. Ole and Sven vote in every election, strictly on issues of economy. For example in the last election, Ole took money from the candidates of both parties. Flushed with cash, Ole went immediately into the local tavern where he occupied the bar stool right next to Sven. "Who did you vote for, Ole?" Sven asked him.

"I voted my conscience," said Ole.

The two men walk blithely and unconcerned through the fields when suddenly a rustling occured in the thicket before them and caught their attention. Finally, a deer!! They must act! And from out of a copse of trees (I have always wanted to use that word) a man inexplicably came running holding his hands straight up and waved them about wildly. He shouts out, "Don't shoot, don't shoot, I'm not a deer!" About what he was doing in the woods I will not here speculate.

But, Ole quickly raised his rifle to his shoulder, aims and fires. The man stumbled as if he had suddenly tripped over a wire and fell to the ground dead. Ole has killed him with a single shot.

"Ole," Sven desperately cries, "Why did you shoot him? The man said he wasn't a deer!"

"Oh, says Ole, "I thought he said he *was* a deer."

I've been telling that joke to my friend Mitch for at least four years now, and at each recounting, we laugh as if it were a new joke. Usually at each telling we are sitting at a local coffee house; these establishments have sprouted up like mushrooms after a good rain since Americans discovered how coffee ought to really taste. And I do love mushrooms. I think these emporiums (ah, I've always wanted to have some use for *that* word) have brought people back out, albeit marginally, into the public sphere. Today, these establishments act as virtual libraries (many customers enter with their laptop computers and their school texts), or virtual offices (many enter with their laptops and their attaché cases), and virtual meeting places (many enter with their laptops on which they immediately connect to their Facebooks and email accounts). Mostly these coffee bars (more upscale and upclass in tone than the traditional coffee shop!) are relatively as quiet as a library. Even now from each other and say not a word, all the while communicating with someone in another virtual office, perhaps sitting in some other coffee house across town. Sometimes patrons sit directly across from each other, not speaking, but chattering back and forth silently on the internet. A few sit in solitude and read quietly, sometimes a book, and at other times a newspaper that may have been left to be recycled by an earlier reader. Still few other patrons actually engage with actual others and have real, live conversations. I am glad they have so much to say. Of course, a great deal of coffee is consumed, some of it carefully disguised as a variety of drinks ending in the letter 'o.'

So, sitting at our regular table, Mitchell and I meet at one particular coffee emporium (there, I've gotten to use the word again!), and I am telling the same old (by this time) Sven and Ole joke again. We sit again at our traditional table, Mitchell with one numerous travel mugs and I with the ceramic mug I carry with me for such gatherings. And when I arrive (yet again) at the final line, we both laugh. The absurd events of the day about which we have read in the newspapers make the joke appear perpetually new. And in our helplessness and despair, we laugh.

How should a joke relate to the world? I suspect a good joke treats the world with considerable irony, situating the absurdity of human behavior in a frame that invites such ironic observation and comment.

Hence, the success and longevity of late night talk show hosts, and *Saturday Night Live,* and other shows of similar genres. But the more absurd the world appears, the more absurd must be the joke. Finally, I suppose, the only good joke is a joke so absurd that it is no longer even funny. And so, though the world is to me more absurd than ever, only the rare joke teller can create the ironic space into which laughter can appear.

I know, I know, I've explained the joke away. It is no longer a joke, and it is no longer funny. Part of what makes a joke viable is its untranslatability into the logic of this world. Or rather, it cannot be explained and remain a joke. The joke must be a bit absurd for it to function as a joke, and the explanation renders the absurd too logical. Why do Mitch and I continue to laugh at this Sven and Ole joke? Because if we didn't laugh, we'd have to cry.

Oh, no. You can't fool me. There ain't no Sanity Clause.

Of course, there is another more dangerous version of this joke that I believe Mitchell and I would never tell to each other, nor would we find space to laugh at it. This version speaks, too, to the times (now hopefully past, though I have my doubts . . .), but the irony here is too real and too tragic. This joke, not funny at all, contains too much truth; none of the names have been changed and no innocence was protected. There were at the time newspapers for which this was not news. And there were newspapers that would not report this news.

A story is told: Two Jews, what difference their names, were walking in Berlin during the rise of Nazi power. Their pants showed the sign of age and wear, and on their heads, they wore hats a bit too worn. On the right breasts of their too-thin coats that were not really sufficient to keep out the cold was pinned the yellow Star of David in the middle of which was written *Juden.* Of course, the two men were thin for in a long time they had not had enough to eat. Today, they were not going to work. Under the Nuremberg Laws, they had been just recently been denied employment; indeed, they were prevented from participating in any aspect of the social order outside of their designation as *Juden.* They walked in the ghetto to which they had been consigned, and spoke to each other only a little. After all, what was there to say? Suddenly, they came upon a poster freshly pasted on wooden planks of a boarded up Jewish bakery. "CAUTION," the sign said. "A lion has escaped from the Berlin Zoo and is now loose in the City. The animal is very dangerous and must be shot on sight." The one man turned to his friend and with a desperation and determination that belied their actual situation, "That's it. I'm leaving town tonight."

The second man—he was a bit taller and so he turned his head slightly down, looked at his friend. "What are so upset about?" he asked. And putting his arm around his friend's shoulders he said, "Relax, you aren't a lion."

"Well, true," said his comrade, "But *you* try to tell them that after you're shot." *Oh, no. You can't fool me. There ain't no Sanity Clause.*

⚏

It is a truism that simply calling something by a label doesn't ensure that the thing is, in fact, the substance identified by the label. Writing a news story does not make the events reported any more or less true. Such confusions, of course, have resulted in not a few respectable jokes and even some great art. 'This is not a pipe,' Magritte labeled his painting that portrayed a pipe. I tell my children that what I do for them is what a good father does, and they tell me, I'm simply a fool. Neither of us is correct, though probably each of us is more accurate than we would ever care to admit. Nor can everything be precisely defined by writing it into a narrative or by assigning it a label; indeed, labels and narratives often serve to obscure. Such confusions often serve political purposes. Ronald Reagan's denial of his engagement in the Iran-Contra affair ended finally in his qualified admission that his administration had engaged in secretive and illegal activity: "A few months ago, I told the American people I did not trade arms for hostages. My heart and my best intentions still tell me that's true, but the facts and the evidence tell me it is not." *Oh, no. You can't fool me. There ain't no Sanity Clause.*

Meaning results from an individual's particular and often idiosyncratic apprehension of narrative. As the Rabbis might say, meaning is not in Heaven but right here on earth. The Democrats say in the newspaper that they are concerned for America; the Republicans say in the newspaper that the Democrats are ruining America. And vice versa. I do not know about what country either is speaking. In fact, I think it is not the country about which they talk at all; they refer to themselves. What is ego but the politician inside each of us? What is the politician but the ego unabashedly externalized.

A story is told:

Once, DeGaulle slipped on a loose rug and fell heavily to the floor. Madame DeGaulle, raising her arms in alarm cried out, "Mon Dieu."

From his place on the floor DeGaulle assured her, "I'm all right dear, but I have told you that when we are alone you must call me by my first name." I read it in the *Daily News*.

A story is told: Two Jews were sitting at a Paris café during the first trial of Captain Albert Dreyfus. One of the men—Alphonse Lambert—was reading the viciously anti-Semitic tabloid, *La Libre Parole* ("Free Speech"), edited by the virulently anti-Semite Edouard Drumont. On November 3, 1894, for example, Drumont wrote concerning the Dreyfus affair, "What a terrible lesson, this disgraceful treason of the Jew Dreyfus!" His alert was clear: Jews are not to be trusted in any position that touched the public weal. Major Esterhazy, later discovered to be the real spy, was then at his assigned post.

Now, sitting at the same table and across from Alphonse was the other Jew—Monsieur Louis Bernard—and he was reading *La Justice*, the paper edited by the Dreyfusard, George Clemençeau, and in whose pages appeared *J'Accuse,* Zola's famous letter in defense of Dreyfus, or at least, in opposition to the guilty verdict rendered against him. In these years, Clemençeau would have been considered a radical! Indeed, as a result of this published accusatory letter Zola himself was tried and convicted for treason, but he managed to escape to Great Britain before his sentence could be executed. Dreyfus, as we know, was found guilty and sent to Devil's Island. Evidence materialized incriminating Major Esterhazy but it was suppressed and he was exonerated of charges brought against him. Albert Dreyfus was then re-accused and re-convicted and returned to Devil's Island. It was not until 1906 that Dreyfus was finally declared innocent, released and reinstated. He served the French in World War I, having survived an assassination attempt in 1908 while attending the funeral of Emile Zola. The would-be assassin was acquitted. Ah, justice, justice thou shalt pursue!

Anyway, the day that I am describing was a beautiful autumn day in Paris, the air warm and fresh, and the leaves all turned to brilliant hues of reds and oranges and yellows. In a day or two, indeed, these leaves would all be gone! The two friends sat quietly at the café, each sipping their espressos, each with his right leg crossed politely over his left knee. Monsieur Bernard (who, you will recall, was reading Clemençeau's publication) looked up from his reading and for the first time, I suppose, noticed his companion's choice of newspaper. In a tone which bordered on panic, he said to his friend, "Alphonse, why are you reading that anti-Semitic libel sheet? Are you some kind of masochist, or worse, a self-hating Jew?"

"Au contraire, mon ami, Louis," said Alphonse, who looked up nonplussed and smiling: "I used to read only the Jewish papers when I would have my coffee. And there I would learn about terrible pogroms taking place in Russia, and the problems of Jewish assimilation in the United States, and the continuing anti-Semitic activities in Germany and Austria that led many Jews to convert if they wanted to prosper. Think about the poor Mendelssohn family! Imagine," Louis shook his head, "how Moshe Mendelssohn, may he rest in peace, must turn in his grave that his grandson became a devout Christian so that he could continue to make such beautiful music. And such magnificent music! His violin concerto could be played at services in shul. Ach! So, as I was saying, I would read these reports in the newspapers and I would get very depressed. Now, as you see, I look at Drumont's *La Libre Parole*, and I see everything so much more clearly. I read here that the Jews control all of the banks, that the Jews dominate the arts, and that the Jews are on the verge of taking over the entire world. On the whole, you know, reading this newspaper makes me feel a whole lot better." *Oh, no. You can't fool me. There ain't no Sanity Clause.*

Not an innocent, neither will Louis be a willing victim. Rather, he assumes his alleged power because he has read about it in the newspaper. If there is no sanity clause in the world, Louis will create sanity for himself! Newspapers tell us what someone wants us to know, but we can also read the newspapers to discover what we want. Despite their rhetoric, newspapers don't tell the truth or order the world as Anna Wulf had hoped in *The Golden Notebook*, but offer only a version of a truth that the Foucauldian ubiquitous and amorphous 'they' construct from the stories to which the tellers have themselves listened and now wish to report. In this way, ironically, newspapers contribute to absurdity even as they aspire to protect us from it. They offer the illusion of order and control, but it is only an illusion! "Humor is reason gone mad," said Groucho, and newspapers pretend to absolute reason. They prevaricate, at worst. At best, they amuse.

The teacher of Helen Keller, Anne Sullivan wrote, "The truth is not wonderful enough to suit the newspapers; so they enlarge upon it, and invent ridiculous embellishments."

And the poet Charles Baudelaire accused, "I am unable to understand how a man of honor could take a newspaper in his hands without a shudder of disgust." Humor results when the pompous aspire to some ethical stance from which even the next day's news reveals the subject to have slipped. "Ozymandias, King of Kings." Oh, how the mighty have fallen!! Ha!

Though essential to a democracy, the democratic standard of any one newspaper is always questionable. All the news that's fit to print? Themselves absurd, newspapers are replete with absurdities. George Bernard Shaw noted that "Newspapers are unable, seemingly to discriminate between a bicycle accident and the collapse of civilization."

Henry David Thoreau held a very low opinion of newspapers. In his journal Thoreau advises, "Do not entertain doubts, if they are not agreeable to you. Send them to the tavern. Do not eat unless you are hungry; there's no need of it. Do not read the newspapers." For Thoreau, the newspapers were filled with idle gossip that was not worth the paper on which it was printed or the time it would take to glance at it. He said, "I do not know, but it is too much to read one newspaper in a week." Of course, a single newspaper contains all of the week's news, though sometimes (but not always) the names do change. American writer A.J. Liebling said, "People everywhere confuse what they read in newspapers with news."

For Thoreau, the news took one away from what was important: the wealth of the day. After all, who wants yesterday's papers, and yet that is what newspapers offer, the events that occurred yesterday. Thoreau bemoaned the time spent on the news asserting that our attention to it was a symptom of the emptiness of our internal lives. "In proportion as our inward life fails, we go more constantly and desperately to the post-office. You may depend on it, that the poor fellow who walks away [from the post office] with the greatest number of letters, proud of his extensive correspondence, has not heard from himself this long while." Sometimes all a person knows is what he reads in the *Daily News.*

A story is told: Once, a foreign journalist came to America to do a series of articles on the quality of life of the workers. After all, the United States has served as the Promised Land for countless dreamers and believers. "Give us your tired and your poor, your sick of heart." Of course, it took the reporter some time to find a worker most of the jobs had been either transferred out of the country or become non-existent in this most recent economic crisis. Finally, at a local Wal-Mart store, the correspondent approached what the company likes to call an associate.

"Do you find your job rewarding?" he asked.

"Absolutely."

"Ah, that is very good. And what is your home like?"

"Oh, it is affordable, spacious, and clean."

Indeed, the journalist was becoming not a little envious. "And during your time off, how do you spend your leisure."

"Oh, we go often as a family to theater or to the opera. Several evenings a month, I attend evening classes, and on the weekends, I spend a great deal of time with my family, my friends and colleagues."

"Do you read the newspapers?"

"Well, of course, I do," the associate responded indignantly, "How else would I know how to answer all of your stupid questions?"

I insist that my students and my children develop some knowledge of American history. With this intent, I assign as reading material Ben Franklin's *Autobiography,* in which Benjamin Franklin represents himself as the quintessential American: industrious, moral, resourceful, ingenious, and civic-minded. Ha! Franklin was a newspaperman, and he knew how to write an editorial. Indeed, he began to make his fortune with the publication of his newspaper and the extant polemical literature, such as *Poor Richard's Almanack,* that derived from it. I mention this because Franklin intended his newspaper to serve some honest, didactic purpose. In his autobiography, written clearly for pedagogical purpose, Franklin writes, "I considered my newspaper also as another means of communicating instruction, and in that view frequently reprinted in it extracts from the *Spectator* and other moral writers, and sometimes little pieces of my own . . . " Franklin meant his newspapers to serve as a means of teaching and providing some moral edification; through the newspaper Franklin meant to create a community based in shared knowledge of mutual concern.

In the eighteenth century, Franklin intended (a little *too* ingenuously, I think) to position his newspaper outside the mainstream fare of daily gossip and libel, and therefore to provide his readers with unbiased and unadulterated information. "In the conduct of my newspaper," he asserts, "I carefully excluded all libeling and personal abuse, which is of late years become so disgraceful in our country." Franklin acknowledged the necessity for a free press, and thus, ever the good businessman, he offered to print *privately* and *for a fee* anything anyone requested. (This recalls to my mind Spinoza's assertion that *anyone* should be allowed to become a teacher as long as that individual assumed the necessary expenses to start up and maintain a school!). Justifying his refusal to engage in printing libelous or salacious material, Franklin avowed, "I could not fill their papers with private altercation in which they had no concern without doing them [his readers] manifest injustice." The newspapers were meant for the intellectual and social edification of the people! And Franklin was concerned with what the material printed in his papers assumed about its audience. Franklin *respected* his readers. Complaining that too many printers did not maintain the same standard, Franklin in his autobiography urged new printers to avoid such insidious and unbecoming practices. Ah, if only the modern press heeded Franklin's admonition, though I think now that might be too much to expect.

Franklin's caution to his fellow printers proves the rule. That is, while he advocated for the moral purity of *his* publication, Franklin's adjuration assured us that the calumny so evident in other journals existed. Franklin meant his publication to be an alternative to the usual fare, refusing to include in its pages whatever smacked of personal abuse and libelous talk. Nothing is but what is not. In this way, Franklin meant to offer his readership important information both entertaining and informative, and to avoid the scandalous stories that degraded the news into hearsay and innuendo. Franklin actually believed in the efficacy of newspapers. Entertaining so that the citizenry would purchase it and informative to ensure the development of a virtuous and informed constituency, Franklin intended his newspaper to serve as a lucrative public service. Of course, one man's libel is another's news, and the distinction between the two often seems a matter of opinion for which purpose courts and prisons became necessary arbiters. Franklin does acknowledge that he (at times) used his paper to further his political ends: he reports in his autobiography that on one occasion he wrote "some spirited remarks . . ." on the dispute then going on between Governor Burnet and the Massachusetts Assembly." But of course, Franklin was always telling the truth! He tells us so in the list of virtues he set as part of his moral regimen to exercise and strengthen.

The ideal of the free press has always had its advocates, but many have expressed dismay at the activities of the newspapers. Benjamin Franklin espoused great faith in the newspaper, but knew its dangers: "If by the liberty of the press were understood merely the liberty of discussing the propriety of public measures and political opinions, let us have as much of it as you please: But if it means the liberty of affronting, calumniating and defaming one another, I, for my part, own myself willing to part with my share of it, whenever our legislators shall please so to alter the law and shall cheerfully consent to exchange my liberty of abusing others for the privilege of not being abused myself."

The Beatle George Harrison (among others) thought it a good day when he read the papers and did not discover his name in them. Harrison must nevertheless have discovered the name of others in his reading of the papers! Franklin's colleague, Thomas Jefferson, held the same conflicted view of the newspapers. Jefferson believed in the necessity of a free press, but recognized how it could be abused. Jefferson is reported to have said, "Advertisements contain the only truths to be relied on in a newspaper." But I know that advertisements are filled with misinformation, and I recommend that *my* daughters not look at the advertisements!

Jefferson placed little credence in any single newspaper but advocated for the presence of a plethora of them so that the citizens of the country might have access to alternative narratives. Jefferson believed passionately in a free press, but grew to despair the degree to which the character and quality of newspapers seemed to him to have declined. In 1807 Jefferson wrote to John Norvell, "Nothing can now be believed which is seen in a newspaper. Truth itself becomes suspicious by being put into that polluted vehicle."

Henry David Thoreau notes continually how newspapers do not tell the truth: "I repeat the testimony of many an intelligent foreigner, as well as my own convictions, when I say, that probably no country was ever ruled by so mean a class of tyrants as, with a few noble exceptions, are the editors of the periodical press in *this* country. And as they live and rule only by their servility, and appealing to the worst, and not the better nature of man, the people who read them are in the condition of the dog that returns to his vomit." Hoo ha! I say.

Thoreau, actually, did subscribe to Horace Greeley's *New York Tribune* (which coincidentally published some of Thoreau's work), though he might not have been a regular reader of it. Thoreau writes in his journal on 2 April, 1853 (though of course, I don't have to believe everything he says there), "The last two *Tribunes* I have not looked at. I have no time to read newspapers. If you chance to live and move and have your being in that thin stratum in which the events which make the news transpire,—thinner than the paper on which it is printed,—then these things will fill the world for you; but if you soar or dive below that plane, you cannot remember nor be reminded of them." And in *Walden*, he declaims, "I am sure that I never read any memorable news in a newspaper. If we read of one man robbed, or murdered, or killed by accident, or one house burned, or one vessel wrecked, or one steamboat blown up, or one cow run over on the Western Railroad, or one mad dog killed, or one lot of grasshoppers in the winter,—we never need read of another. One is enough . . .

To a philosopher all *news,* as it is called, is gossip, and they who edit and read it are old women over their tea." After all, all the news that's fit to print must fit into so many purchased pages of newsprint. Or, as Seinfeld wonders, "It's amazing that the amount of news that happens in the world every day always just exactly fits the newspaper." I have myself often noticed how the news is usually so spare on weekends! As a text the newspaper becomes available for deconstruction. Why this story and not that one? Why here and not there? Why him and not her? Adlai Stevenson said, "Accuracy to a newspaper is what virtue is to a lady; but a newspaper can always print a retraction." These retractions usually appear deeply buried in a corner of an inner page. The news must be news to someone, though whether the story is reliable is always uncertain. Always it is news though it is rarely new. And somewhere what is printed becomes true.

A story is told: Two Jews, Yossel Klein and Feyvel Davidovich, were very good friends, but one day, over a glass of mint brandy, they suffered a disagreement. They agreed to go to the house of their Rabbi—the wisest man in the town—and present their case before him. The Rabbi, they knew, would know the correct thing and decide who was right.

When they got to the Rabbi's house, he was deep in study; his wife sat quietly in the corner of the room repairing a torn sock. Yossel explained to the Rabbi why they had him, and the Rabbi patiently put aside his book and looked at the two men intently. "Okay," he said to Yossel, "what is your argument?" Yossel spoke for five full minutes laying out the details of his case.

When he had finished, the Rabbis said, "Well, clearly, *you* are right." And then the Rabbi turned to Feyvel. "Well, now let me hear *your* argument," and Feyvel launched into a ten-minute disquisition outlining his case in great detail. When he had finished, the Rabbi lifted his eyebrows and said, "Well, clearly *you* are right!"

Upon hearing this, the Rabbi's wife who had sat quietly darning his socks but who had been listening to the conversation, looked up and said to her husband, "But dear, though you are the wisest of men, how can both men be right?"

Stroking his beard, the rabbi said, "You know, *you* are right, too." The newspapers are never accurate but always right. We must choose the story we would believe, knowing that though *we* are right, so too is the person who disagrees with us. It is absurd to presume our story as the only one. "Why weren't the original indictment papers placed in my portfolio," Rufus Firefly demands of his adjutant. "You didn't think they were important? You realize I had my dessert wrapped in those papers!" Newspapers do serve some honest purpose: where else to put the fish and chips?

But I think I know what Thoreau means; the world doesn't change much daily, and the news in the pages of the papers merely announces what has already happened and about which little can be done. Right now, as I write thousands of barrels of oil are pouring into the Gulf of Mexico from a gushing British Petroleum wellhead that sprang a leak after on oil rig explosion. With no end to the spill in view, I sit so patiently wondering where I read *this* story before. I do read the news, but I don't have to do so to know that wars are taking place and are being even now planned; I don't have to read the papers to know about the horrors of Darfur, or the most recent exemplars of injustices practiced on peoples by their governments. I read the papers nonetheless, smack my forehead with my open hand, look upwards and sigh, "I could have had a V-8!" I too often play Alphonse to someone's Louis. Not too much changes, and the newspapers report this stasis.

A story is told: Two women are walking home after a long day at the factory. They are weary from the labor, and though they work a full week, they make barely enough to pay their household bills and put food on their tables. They are anxious and guilty about the hours they must spend away from home and the children. The rents are too high, and food and clothing expensive. They are heading to pick up their young sons and daughters at the day care center to which the children must go after they are dismissed from school. The latest economic crisis has only increased their hardship, and they worry that a cut-back at the plant might eliminate their jobs. Selma sighs. "Gertie," she says, ""what exactly is the difference exactly between the Republicans and the Democrats?"

"Oh," Gertie says, "that's easy. Under the Republicans, man exploits man, but under the Democrats it is vice versa." I read it in the *Daily News*.

I read the newspapers assiduously nonetheless. This practice does situate me in the world in which I live, absurd though that world may appear. As I have said elsewhere (a phrase popular among academics and used for shameless self-promotion), I daily check the headlines online from the *New York Times*, peruse them periodically during the day; the news too often weighs too heavily on my consciousness. Despite his disclaimer, Thoreau also followed daily events and kept himself informed, and responded at times in action and in writing. His famous night in jail was a response to his opposition to the illegal Mexican War begun by President Polk about which he must have read in the newspapers. The Thoreau family home served as a stop on the Underground Railroad, and we are aware of at least one instance when a runaway slave hid for an evening at the cabin at Walden Pond. The women of Concord met at his cabin to discuss issues of abolition. Thoreau's ideal may have been to stay uninformed, but it was his character not to remain so. Thoreau does not always follow his own admonition concerning the news.

For example, you might read in his journal his heated reporting of the hanging of John Brown in 1859. In his journal entries from 19-22 October, 1859, Henry David addresses vigorously John Brown's failed assault on the armory at Harper's Ferry. Now admittedly, this was a very complex situation, and Brown was a complex, and even unknown man. Here, I do not mean to address Brown's actions. Rather, here I want to note Thoreau's ire, indeed, his fury at the various agencies whose advocacy of slavery made necessary Brown's acts and whose assessment of Brown had attributed his actions to madness and not to principle. To Thoreau, it was the world that was insane and not John Brown though the newspapers suggested otherwise. I want here to note Thoreau's thorough respect for the character of John Brown, whose commitment to the oppressed was total, but whose actions appeared absurd to a calloused and immoral world. Thoreau writes, "I know that there have been a few heroes in the land, but no man has ever stood up in America for the dignity of human nature so devotedly, persistently, and so effectively as this man." Thoreau does not condone Brown's act, but neither does he condemn it. Rather, Thoreau accuses the newspapers of ignorance and cowardice for the story they had constructed for the readers: "Prominent and influential editors, accustomed to deal with politicians, men of an infinitely lower grade, say, in their ignorance, that [Brown] acted 'on the principle of revenge.' They do not know the man. They must enlarge themselves to conceive of him . . . they have got to conceive of a man of ideas and of principle, hard as it may be for them . . . of a man who did not wait till he was personally interfered with or thwarted in some harmless business before he gave his life to the cause of the oppressed." The baseness of the media and the politicians is no less offensive today than in Thoreau's time. I am no less appalled, and no less ashamed of my government officials and my own helplessness than was Thoreau. We live even now in debased times. Just read the papers!

Thoreau was indignant that a man of principle, a man whose abhorrence of slavery and hatred of the slaveholder led him to engage in extreme measures, could be so little understood in a country begun by the Declaration of Independence and detailed by the Constitution. Thoreau was disgusted by the complete moral failure of the newspapers to accurately depict the character of John Brown and to offer public support for this hero. "I wish to correct the tone and some of the statements of the newspapers responding the life and character and last action of John Brown. The newspapers seem to ignore, or perhaps they are really ignorant of, the fact that there are at least as many as one or two individuals to a town throughout the North who think much as I do about him and his enterprise . . ." But the newspapers vilified John Brown whom Thoreau likened to Christ, and had transformed Brown's acts into those of a mad man. "I have read all the newspapers I could get within a week, and I do not remember in them a single expression of sympathy for these men." And yet, to Thoreau, there was in America no one like John Brown and the men who had joined in his holy quest; only *their* deaths gave evidence of *lives* lived. Brown and the men who fought with him were the true patriots. "Franklin,—Washington,—they were let off without dying; these were merely missing one day." No, only John Brown by his death has taught us how to live.

I do not have to read the news to be reminded of the venality of the human race. Of that, I am daily well-assured in active living, but I suppose I read the newspapers to remain convinced, and to act surprised at the most recent act of socially egregious behavior. And why would I so masochistically immerse myself to such iniquity? I suppose it is because without such news I would have no material for the jokes. These tales depend upon a world that does not make sense, and the newspapers continue to convince me that this is, alas, the world in which I live. This is no Golden Age. I need the jokes to establish some distance from that world and to protest against its insanity.

[furioso] Newspapers report the crimes, but they do not stop them; they report the lies that sometimes they expose, but they just don't seem to be able to prevent the lying in the first place. Everybody speaks for the nation, but every one of those who speak, speaks for a different nation, I think. And there is a newspaper and print media for each of them, (certainly the advantage of democracy), and none of them have stopped the dissemination of duplicity that oppresses the country, and some have actually perpetuated it. For example, I have read that *Human Events*, the National Conservative Weekly since

1944 (their blurb!), "asked a panel of fifteen conservative scholars and public policy leaders to help compile a list of the Ten Most Harmful Books of the 19th and 20th Centuries." Okay. I have quoted this post exactly because I don't want you to think I am making this up!! As if the list itself isn't the silliest thing in the world, as if there is a competent idea inhering to the whole notion of this list. The Number One most harmful book, as you might expect from the editors of *Human Events*, is *The Communist Manifesto,* by Karl Marx. Second, (though I don't know if it is a close second or not!), was Adolf Hitler's *Mein Kampf.* Third, as you can guess given the direction here, is *The Quotations of Chairman Mao,* and in fourth place is Alfred Kinsey's *The Kinsey Report.* I wonder if the scholars responsible for this list of the most harmful books of the 19th and 20th century were truly appalled by the subject of the Kinsey Report, or were angered at being discovered in their sexual preferences and peccadilloes, or even by their lack of them? Recent reports suggests that our contemporary politicians know a great deal about the matter of the Kinsey Report though they have tended to deny and even to legislate against any such knowledge.

Thus far the list, silly as it is, is also horribly predictable. And remarkably limited. I mean, the *Protocols of Zion*, a text that has led to not a few pogroms, to untold massacres of Jews, and that has sponsored a considerable host of other vicious anti-Semitic acts, did *not* make the list! Go figure! The publishing of the *Protocols* was brought to us by that American icon Henry Ford. I wonder: once a book makes the list, is it more or less harmful? Shouldn't we all be required to read these books that the editors declare harmful so that we would know what ideas to avoid? Or to at least to understand what a harmful idea might look like. Newspapers practice a similar censorship. They only print the news that they (again, the omnipresent, Foucauldian 'they') believe benefits me and incidentally strengthens them. I am reminded here of Dylan's plaint, "When I was in Missouri/They would not let me be/I had to leave there in a hurry/I only saw what they let me see." So the Human Events judges (can I really refer to these fools as 'judges?') read the books no one else should read.

But when I arrived at the book nominated in fifth place, I ceased to chuckle. For on that list right underneath *The Quotations of Chairman Mao*, and right above Marx's *Das Kapital* (I assume Volume I, though this is not made clear in the list by *Human Events)* is John Dewey's *Democracy and Education.* Ah, they fool me to the top of my bent!. Happening suddenly upon this item in the list, I began to understand the condition known as apoplexy. John Dewey's *Democracy and Education* is an eloquently argued advocacy for a social system constructed from the foundation of an educational establishment in which social justice and individual contentment co-depend and co-exist. Few cared more about democracy than John Dewey (someone from the Christian Right should read his essay "Democracy and Christianity"), and no one held education in higher regard as essential to democracy than John Dewey. Without an educational system based in *Democracy and Education*, without a social system advocated in *Democracy and Education*, then all of those harmful books wouldn't be known as harmful. They'd be permanent policy!

A story is told: A terrible thunderstorm raged one evening, and little Martha rose terrified from her bed and ran to her parents' bedroom. "Daddy, daddy," she cried, shaking her sleepy father awake. "Daddy, why is it thundering?"

Now, her father was a wise and kind man, a professor of journalism, in fact, and so he sat up in the bed and nestled his daughter in his arms. "Well, dear," he began, "every time someone tells a big lie on earth, heaven gets very angry, and it thunders."

The girl's sniffles quieted down. "But daddy, I don't understand. It's late at night now and everyone is asleep."

"Ah yes," her patient father answered, hugging his daughter close and staring out at the storm, "but it is about this time that *Human Events* goes to press."

/scherzando/ George Santayana remarked that he who does not learn from history is doomed to repeat it, and Karl Marx has said that history repeats itself, the first time as tragedy and the second time as farce. In these times, both men are right, and often when the newspapers run a story, they need only change the names to protect the guilty. At our chosen coffee house, Mitchell, my friend and colleague and party in silliness, order our coffee and when possible, we head for the same table. We refer to this location as the Feedback Corner, and we offer unsolicited advice and comfort to other customers and passers-by. Mostly we amuse ourselves. Sometimes the space is already occupied, and then we reluctantly choose another available table and glare at what we describe as the usurpers, and our conversation remains somewhat uneasy until our regular place becomes available and we move to it. Neither one of us is exceptionally comfortable with too much dislocation. But we do like to talk, and the world

offers so much with which to horrify and amuse.

Mitchell and I usually begin with a review of the events of the day that we have culled from the newspapers. Fortunately, the Republicans are always saying something absurd that affords us some early levity. Here in Wisconsin, the two Republicans running in the primary for the U.S. Senate agree with Republican Joe Barton's characterization of the escrow fund the President has demanded BP Oil set aside to address the catastrophic environmental and economic disaster the explosion of its oil rigged has caused to the Gulf Coast as a "shakedown." I suppose that these politicians believe that only people and not corporations must be held accountable for their misdeeds. The Rabbis say, "If I am answerable for the care of a thing, it is I that render possible the injury that it may do. If I render possible part of that injury I must make restitution for that injury as he that rendered possible the whole of that injury." Take that, Joe Barton!

I recall that Massachusetts senator Charles Sumner was almost beaten to death by his Senate colleague, South Carolina Representative Preston Brooks in 1856. Ultimately, the argument was over the issue of slavery, which Sumner detested. Quite recently, before a stunned nation (alas, I am crediting a morality to the electorate that may not really exist) a South Carolinian Senator interrupted the President of the United States in the midst of his publicly televised State of the Union Address. "You lie," he called out from his seat in the audience. I could not help but wonder if the Southern Senator would have so spoken if the President had been Caucasian? Once as tragedy... One other Republican representative who will remain nameless to protect the guilty was reported to have referred to members of our present governmental leaders as 'pigs,' whom we have to remove from Washington if we are to ever 'take our country back.' I am certain that both these members of Congress (and not a few others whose sexual and economic peccadilloes fill the front pages of our newspapers) will expect their children's teachers to instill respect for others and for the United States to which by law these children must daily pledge allegiance. Second time as farce.

Mitchell and I note reports in the newspapers that the conservative Republican Board of Regents in Texas in the most recent version of their school curriculum removed Thomas Jefferson from a list of those whose writings inspired Revolution. I can't imagine what they are going to do to explain the authorship of the Declaration of Independence! But perhaps this will not be too big an issue because at the directive of the same Texas Board of Regents Jefferson's role in American history will be downplayed because this unpatriotic

American coined the term 'separation of church and state,' and therefore, was complicit in expelling mention of God from the schools. And you know what happens to a Godless nation! According to the new history standards, the word *capitalism* has been replaced by 'free enterprise' and the inaugural speech of Confederate President Jefferson Davis will be studied alongside that of Abraham Lincoln. Fortunately, in the wonderful system of free enterprise, the text book companies remain unconcerned. New technologies makes it easy for them to custom-tailor textbooks for each state, and therefore, the demands of the new Texas curriculum can be easily adapted (and adopted, as the case may be) to ensure vigorous and continued text book sales. History certainly need not affect the integrity of history textbook marketing.

I assume that the recent attacks from the Christian Right on evolution will certainly have their effect on the content of the Texas school books. I recall that several years ago the national newspapers were filled with reports that the School Board of Kansas mandated that though high school students must understand major evolutionary concepts, the School Board also insisted that students be instructed that Darwin's theory—which suggests that all life had a common origin, and that natural chemical processes and not God at Creation fashioned the building blocks of life—had been challenged in recent years by fossil evidence and molecular biology. I have not seen their research. It did not appear in the newspapers, alas! No doubt, Texas will soon follow Kansas' lead.

The Washinton Post runs an annual contest in which the newspaper challenges readers to take a common word and change one letter in it to create a new word. Contestants must then give that new word a definition. The year that I learned about the competition the winning entry was *ignoranus*, someone who is both stupid and an asshole. Another of my favorites from that year was *dopeler* effect, the tendency of stupid ideas to seem smarter when they come at you rapidly.

And speaking of expulsions and revisions: In this free country one can print almost anything that isn't expressly (and obviously) libelous and not even have to pay for it. For this I suppose I am grateful, but in this moment of ecological crisis, shouldn't greater attention be paid to the quantities of papers and ink that must be used to publish material. I don't know if Ann Coulter counts herself as a Republican, but she certainly announces herself a Christian and a Conservative. In a footnote on the third page of her book, *Godless: The Church of Liberalism*, Coulter writes, without irony I suspect, (which means that her assertion is not intended to be in the least bit humorous), "Throughout this book, I often refer to Christians and Christianity because I am a Christian and I have a firmly good idea of what that term means, but the term is intended to include anyone who subscribes to the Bible of the God of Abraham, including Jews and others." How kind of her to include Jews as subscribers to the Bible that speaks so often of Jews. Mitchell and I, both Jews, are relieved however, for we know firsthand the consequences for Jews when someone questions their allegiance to Christian belief. If this note appears on the bottom of page three, then what would possibly justify continuing on to the top of page four? What editor approved the publication of such nonsense and with what animus was it sanctioned for printing?

"Relax, you aren't a lion."

"Well, true," said his comrade, "But *you* try to tell them that after you're shot."

≢

I jokingly mentioned to Mitchell that I had heard a conservative commentator on one of those seemingly ubiquitous right wing talk shows discussing his ideas concerning the complex politics of the Middle East. First, he launched into a scathing critique of the present administration's attempt to effect some negotiation between the Israelis and the Palestinians. Of course, he attributed the entire mess to Democratic administrations dating back even to Andrew Jackson, and then he lamented, again without a touch of irony, "I can't understand the difficulty of the process. I don't understand why the Arabs and the Jews can't learn to live together like good Christians!" But the report seemed so accurate to him that Mitchell didn't even laugh. First time as tragedy. . . .

≢

Mitchell loves to read history. Newspapers often become history, though it seems lately that too often they ignore it, and so in our discussion after we have reduced the newspapers to a few jokes, Mitchell turns to the latest book he is reading accompanied by a small lecture he has prepared for my intellectual edification and growth. In those books, Mitchell discovers the stories too often absent from the papers. In Jewish culture, these stories are referred to as midrash, and they are answers to the questions unresolved and even unasked in the text. We know that every word printed in a text takes up the space another word might have taken. There is always a different word and a different meaning available. Even in newspapers. Interestingly, there is usually much more truth in the stories than in the facts. After all, the facts are only words; the stories are life.

For the past several years, Mitchell has chosen books addressing the civil rights struggle in the United States, a topic that particularly interests him. One of his favorite reads in the past several years has been *An American Insurrection: James Meredith and The Battle of Oxford, Mississippi, 1962*, by William Doyle, and at most of our meetings (and right after I retell the Sven and Ole joke), Mitchell repeats his favorite selection from the book. He recites: "Kennedy sent the United States Army to Mississippi to ensure the integration of Old Miss, the University of Mississippi." Mitchell repeats: "*The President sent the U.S. Army!*" Mitchell wants me to be awed by the immensity of the force, and I am always dutifully impressed. Mitchell continues, raising the index finger on his right hand and with the slightest twinkle in his eye, "But the law enforcement officials in Mississippi were not to be cowed by this envoy of the U.S. Government. To confront the invading forces, the state of Mississippi, under order from their governor, Ross Barnett, sent *six* state Highway patrol cars to prevent these foreign intruders from entering the state of Mississippi. And as would-be vigilantes or a klavern of the KKK out on some terrorist mission, the Mississippi Highway Patrol rode out armed, with their sirens screaming and their lights flashing to forestall what they claimed was an illegal invasion of their land, and to protect their racist ideology and the purity of their women." The highway patrol officers with their cars blocking the road to Oxford stood (I imagine) lined up before their vehicles with the hand of each placed threateningly on their pistols, and awaited the confrontation with the Yankee soldiers, some of whom, Mitchell suspects, were Southern and others of whom, Mitchell assures me, were African American.

Suddenly, from down the road came the U.S. Army—(Mitchell

quotes here from Doyle's text. He keeps a copy of the list in his billfold)—"a convoy of 161 vehicles, led by two sweeper scout Jeeps, followed by fifty patrol Jeeps. Following them, were small quarter ton trucks, followed by heavy trucks at the rear. Machine guns were mounted on the trucks." As my grandmother might say, "*Vey iz mir!*" When the highway patrol, claiming their authority from the Governor of the State, barred the troops entrance into the State of Mississippi and ordered the United States Army to turn about and return from whence they came (but not in those words), Major LeVan climbed on top of the communications truck, placed himself at the trigger of a .50 caliber machine gun and pointed the gun at the patrolman. Behind him was the United States Army and dozens of guns immediately aimed and poised at the Highway Patrol.

I interrupt Mitchell at this point usually and tell him I can't help thinking of Barney Fife, the deputy sheriff in Mayberry.

He chuckles, "Naturally!" and continues on with the story.

Major LeVan moved to the microphone: "I represent the President of the United States. You have two minutes to move your asses out of the way, or I'll blow you off the road. Starting now." Then the Major started to count backwards. The highway patrolmen stood still, and Major LeVan ordered his men to prepare to move forward as he continued his countdown. The roar of the army vehicle engines filled the air, though I suspect the highway patrol cars had been shut down and did not add to the din. Regardless, I don't think they would have been heard over the army's roar. When Major LeVan reached zero, as would the best cavalry officer, he waved his arm and the convoy moved forward at a somewhat accelerated speed toward the highway patrol blockade. At the last minute the officers raced to their cars, climbed in and sped rapidly away, with their tailpipes pulled up beneath the two rear tires. And the U.S. Army entered the State of Mississippi. First time as tragedy . . .

But Mitchell isn't finished because the story isn't done.

Unbelievably, when the army finally reached Oxford, they were met by yet another highway patrol blockade. This time Major LeVan, clearly out of patience, gave them no time, but ordered the "deuce-and a half- truck" to push the police cruiser out of the way. The Army truck crashed into the abandoned patrol car and continued on its way as the highway patrol officers stood cowed, mouths hung open, somewhere a good distance from their now moving vehicles. And now the United States Army entered Oxford, Mississippi. Second time as farce.

And having told this story again, Mitchell grins, and says, "The

Civil War never ended. It just went on hold." Today, 147 years after the Emancipation Proclamation, 145 years after end of the Civil War, fifty-six years after Brown vs. Board of Education, and forty-five years after the Civil Rights Act, and despite the election of an African-American President, racism thrives in the United States.

A story is told: A young African American young man, college educated and smartly dressed, applied for a job in a technology company in the state capital, Jackson, Mississippi. "Can you read English, French, Chinese and Spanish?"

"Yes I can," the young man answered proudly.

"Very good," the human resources person said, nodding his head. "And can you play the trumpet?" he asked.

"Yes, I can," the young man answered. "In fact, I can play not only the trumpet but the piano as well. A few friends and myself have a small jazz band."

"Ah, very good," the interviewer said. "And can you ride a bicycle."

"Well, as a matter of fact, I can, indeed, ride a bicycle."

"Oh, well, in that case, I'm sorry, we cannot hire you. You see, we're looking for someone that can't ride a bicycle!" Oh no, there is no sanity clause!

These jokes are our protest, ineffective though they finally may be against the discrepancy between the way things are and the way we believe they ought to be.

A somewhat different version of the same joke is told, and it also is not very funny.

A story is told: Once, the beloved Chief Rabbi of Moscow died and a number of prominent clergymen applied for the job. Joseph Stalin, perhaps you have heard of him, insisted that he be shown the names of all of the applicants. And so his secretary handed him the list of candidates for Chief Rabbi of Moscow which Stalin then proceeded to read: "Abramovitch... Rabinowitz... Simeonovitch... Isaakimov,..." Suddenly, Stalin jumped out of his chair and with fury in his voice bellowed, "What is the meaning of this? All of these men are Jews..." Not according to Ann Coulter! Would it were so!!

Second time as farce. I love it when American history comes alive, and so I was delighted when I read in the newspapers a report of the slight mishap that occurred not too many years ago during a hunting expedition enjoyed by one of our elected high officials. The shooting of Harry Whittington, an Austin lawyer, by his 'good friend' and our Vice President Dick Cheney, recalled to me the duel between Alexander Hamilton and Aaron Burr that forever changed the course, nay, even the very nature of America. The first time as tragedy. Reading *The New York Times* drew me to the papers of the early 19th century, when apparently, the news of the event was also slow to be made public. Burr's political career was ultimately ended by the duel, though apparently there has been little repercussion for Cheney after his involvement in the later event. How the worm has turned. Second time as farce.

The vice president of the United States shot a man one Sunday while he was on a hunting expedition. That is, the vice president missed the quail and hit his friend. With a rifle. A weapon. Of mass destruction. Ah, but who really cares? Better to obsess and spend millions and millions of precious dollars on the relatively harmless sexual peccadilloes of Bill Clinton who once lied about getting a blow job.

That is, while American soldiers fight and die in Iraq and Afghanistan and who knows where they will be sent next; while Americans suffer from lack of adequate health care and educational opportunities; while the American economy deteriorates regularly; while nuclear weapons proliferate, and we remain without a clue how to responsibly respond; while the trade deficit grows dangerously large, and miners die as a result of neglect and lack of oversight; while the homeless from the tragedy in New Orleans run out of options; while the cost of our misguided policies require cuts in spending for education and social security and pensions, the Vice-President went quail hunting and shot his friend. With a gun. With a weapon of mass destruction.

WHAT DO YOU MEAN THE VICE-PRESIDENT OF THE UNITED STATES SHOT HARRY WHITTINGTON, AN AUSTIN LAWYER, AND THEN WENT HOME TO SUPPER? Shouldn't the papers have called out the National Guard? Aaron Burr had to flee to his daughter's home in South Carolina following the duel, though eventually he did return to complete his term as vice president. Finally, he came to a disgraced end. But Cheney? Second time as farce . . .

The sadness is that this event is another blip on a radar screen, and everyone is either asleep or waiting distractedly for someone's privates to be made public. I think politics is all about denial; he who denies the best wins. Newspapers print these vociferous and voluminous denials. It is reported (with not a little levity) that Cheney reflected that his action proves the validity of the Administration's foreign policy: shoot first and ask questions later.

A story is told: Vice-President Cheney and the Secretary of Defense, Donald Rumsfeld, were out hunting one day. Perhaps it was a weekend when fortunately the world was at rest and there was not much to read in the newspapers. A deer sauntered through a copse of trees and the two men fired almost simultaneously. Bambi slumped to the ground dead. The two men turned and slapped each other on the back as men would do. Rumsfeld, resentfully of slightly lower rank, told the vice president to wait with the deer while he went off to find someone to help carry their trophy back. Not a few minutes later, Rumsfeld returned with some under-secretaries. Cheney was standing alone, and the deer was nowhere in sight. "Where's the deer?" asked Rumsfeld.

"What deer?" said Cheney.

"Wait a minute," says Rumsfeld, "didn't we both come out here to hunt together?"

"Yes, we did, my friend."

"And didn't we both see a deer coming through that copse of woods?" said Rumsfeld.

"Yes, we certainly did, Don."

"And . . . and didn't we both shoot that deer?"

"Yes we did."

"And didn't I say I would go and get some help, and didn't I leave you here for just a few minutes to guard the deer?"

"Yes, you did."

"So," said Rumsfeld, "where's the deer?"

"What deer?"

Another story is told: It seems that Thomas Jefferson, Abraham Lincoln and George Bush found themselves in Hell. One day, sitting about having a cup of instant coffee (one of the punishments in Hell) they were discussing their current situation. Jefferson said, "I believed heartily in liberty, and I wrote the Declaration of Independence, but I was too blind and selfish to free even my own slaves. That is why I am here, in Hell."

Abraham Lincoln said, "I was the President during the most difficult days of the Republic, and I think by my actions the Union was saved. But I too often undertook actions that violated the very constitution I was meant to serve. I waited too long to free the slaves, and I think my actions caused great suffering. And that is why I am here." The two then turned to the third occupant of their table. He sat rigidly upright with his arms tightly crossed on his chest. "I am George Bush, son of George H.W. Bush. I am a graduate of Yale University, and a two-term President of the United States. This place is not Hell and I am not here."

≈

I engage in an extraordinary journey when I listen to the second movement of Beethoven's 9th Symphony. I do not think I say here anything itself remarkable, for my words lack real weight before the reality of this symphony. To my mind, the 9th is one of the world's most magnificent creations. And the journey through this second movement of Beethoven's creation, filled as it seems to me with struggle and triumph, with pain and joy, with ugliness and beauty, challenges and stimulates me, and fills me with awe and wonder. Hearing it my spirits are raised.

But no, I do not intend to offer some inadequate and uninformed analysis of this second movement; there are voices far, far more eloquent than mine to serve this purpose. Rather, I want to note here that every time I hear the opening measures of the second movement, I am reminded of the opening moments of the Huntley-Brinkley report that appeared on NBC news during the 1960s and early 1970s.

I do not know who chose the theme music for this program, but clearly it was someone who understood the nature of the news and meant the music to set the tone for the reporting of it. Whoever chose this music understood the substance and consequence of the news report, and to prepare for its presentation opted for the dramatic, opening measures that culminate in the portentous beats of the tympani drum. The news reported by Chet Huntley and David Brinkley mirrored the journey of the second movement, filled with struggle and triumph, with pain and joy, with ugliness and even beauty. And the close of the movement with its furious driving rhythm accompanied by the pounding of the tympani drums served well as the conclusion of the news program, a fitting end to the arduous, climactic journey on which the symphony and the news had engaged us. The second movement of the 9th Symphony by Ludwig van Beethoven was the perfect frame for this production. At the end of both, I was relieved, even exhausted, and glad for the moment of rest.

I cannot help but compare the solemnity with which the news was treated then to the superficialities and silliness that accompanies it now. If history occurs first as tragedy and then as farce, then the news reporting today exemplifies common ribaldry. Then, the news seemed significant and important, and reporting it required dignity and a sense of solemnity. Today, regardless of the content, the tone is glib or melodramatic (which might be the same thing), the newscasters insubstantial and undignified, and too often, crude and insensitive. I don't know that these performers know anything about what they report, and what they report partakes of little matter. News has become just another reality TV show, manipulating events to entertain and not to inform, designed to attract viewers and hence, advertising dollars. These so-called news programs address themselves to those who would not journey, but remain content with fast food take-out and home delivery. If the news has not changed, then its means of being reported has undergone a precipitous and somewhat dangerous decline. Groucho once said, "I read in the newspapers they are going to have thirty minutes of intellectual stuff on television every Monday from 7:30 p.m. to 8:00 p.m. to educate America. They couldn't educate America if they started at 6:30." *Oh, no. You can't fool me. There ain't no Sanity Clause.*

/nobilmente/ Beethoven is no longer considered suitable as introduction or conclusion to the news of the day. This is regrettable. "At any rate," Thoreau writes, "I do not think it is sane to spend one's whole life talking or writing about this matter, and I have not done so. A man may have other affairs to attend to." I go myself now to other affairs.

FOURTH MOVEMENT
Theme and Variations

|affetuoso| My mother is losing her memory. She forgets many things, all the normal things: names, faces and places. They say it is irreversible dementia. She occupies her room passively and somewhat distractedly, listening to an endless loop of Frank Sinatra given to her by one of her grandchildren. The nurses turn the player on in the morning and shut it off at the end of the day. My mother adored Sinatra, loved to brag to us of having been a bobbysoxer screaming in adolescent sexual frenzy (not her words) at the sight and sound of Ol' Blue Eyes. It is hard to think of my mother in this way when I visit her now, but I am satisfied to consider that once she experienced great joy. I sit by her quietly and hold her hand while she hums the tunes she once sang flawlessly. She has now forgotten the lyrics. She doesn't always remember me.

Over her years, my mother has suffered insuperable loss. More than fifty years ago, her beloved older sister succumbed to complications of heart disease. It was the early years of open heart surgery, and my aunt never made it off the operating table. At her sister's death, my mother died a bit as well. Nothing could replace the loss of her sister, and nothing could fill the emptiness my mother experienced. We were always guilty. Ten years ago her husband—my father— died and left her alone. For as long as I had known them, my parents lived in contentious disharmony. She would peck at his scabs incessantly with a mercilessness that drove him into a sense of inadequacy and great unhappiness—and his agony drove him out to a life of continuous and hard work. All of *her* unhappiness, much of which certainly preceded and had little to do with him, she ascribed to *his* behaviors. He bore a very heavy load, I think, and when she lost him to death, she was left to carry the burden herself. I think she was not all that strong.

Though longevity exists in her genes, she is the last of her family of origin yet alive. Her children and grandchildren are far-flung and all but lost to her. Her friends, some of whom she earlier abandoned for some unspoken reasons that had probably more to do with her bitterness than their relationship, are now gone. Those to whom she clung have fallen victim to disease and death. But when I narrate her past for her she remembers none of the names. She has lost most of her earthly attachments. There is nothing in her life except the vacancy of her aloneness.

I note that my memory lacks some consistency as well. But rather than dementia, I blame economy. My thought processes work just fine, thank you, and for the most part I can remember all of the characters in Dostoevsky's *The Brothers Karamazov*. My sentences roll literarily on, and I can yet follow the prose of Henry James, George Eliot, Philip Roth's later Zuckerman novels, and the poetry of Shakespearean drama. I can listen equally attentively to the dialogue and silences of Harold Pinter's plays. I can sing along with a good part of Bob Dylan's collected works without having to look up the lyrics anywhere, and I know that Gertrude Ederle was the first woman to swim the English Channel in 1926. I am very aware that there are a myriad more 'things' I remember and can call up in an instant anytime and anywhere.

But there are things I don't remember, and I can't remember some of the things I've forgotten. And I consider that I am not so much forgetting my life as conserving its energy; there are things I need not now recall to compose a narrative of my life. I remembered Ederle's achievement because her story figures in a book about sports that I received as a gift for my Bar Mitzvah and that I read over and over, and then reread again! It was an oversized book with a brown cloth binding, and it was filled with text and pictures of America's greatest sports heroes. I was then a great sports fan. Long ago, I gave that book to a student hoping its subject matter would inspire him to learn to read it, though I have long since forgotten his name. Nevertheless, for the most part I know how to recover what I think I've forgotten; I have the capacity to maintain the integrity of my narrative.

Perhaps forgetting is also a letting go. There are things that are no longer basic to instant recall. Memory here is not a quantity but a process of organizing what one requires into some narrative. One needn't be suffering from dementia to lack narrative power, and loss of memory doesn't necessarily mean dementia. Sometimes forgetting might be characterized as wisdom.

Though the frustration I sometimes hear in my mother's voice speaks of neither economy nor wisdom; she has lost too much, and perhaps there are no longer enough resources available to make narrative possible. In her face, rests a frightened sense of bewilderment. *|agitato|* Freud says somewhere that what is forgotten—what remains unconscious—is unalterable and unvarying, but it remains, of course, unknown. It is not remembered. Memory here may be unknowable but not without influence. It undergirds what I think I know and determines the contour of consciousness. But what is recovered from memory—what is remembered—is immediately subject to a 'wearing-away.' Unearthed, memories are subject to natural erosion and decomposition, and the reliability of such memories becomes suspect.

I think humans demand narrative. We search for remnants of the past to help us construct the story, but alas, these shards are only remnants. By the very nature of their form, memories are incomplete; they arise out of narrative and possess meaning as they inform narrative. Finally, memories must conform to narrative structure. And if my unconscious can never be known, then my actions are too often if not an attempt to remember, certainly the result of forgetting. We discover only what we intend to discover. Memory is motive-driven. Memories begin in the present, and they do not recreate the past so much as invent it. Memory is the footprint of the present in the past. Memory restores. Narrative restores. But it is, of course, all fiction.

Perhaps the writing of memory is critical to our sense of self: the evocation of the narrative. It is the words that are human—even if sometimes they come from beyond the grave, or even from Hell. Words preserve. Ulysses calls to his men:

Think of your breed; for brutish ignorance
Your mettle was not made; you were made men
To follow after knowledge and excellence.

These lines from Dante's *Inferno*, remembered by Primo Levi in Auschwitz, offered him the strength to go on. There from Hell, Ulysses and Levi urged humankind to continue to quest for knowledge, even though its pursuit may destroy and lead to death. Ulysses' *words* gave life meaning, and though Levi lived in the camps as if already dead, in Ulysses' words Levi can remember what it is that made him human. Language sustains. Memory in language sustains.

|dolce| "Oyfn Pripetchik" is a Yiddish song about a *cheder*, a school in which young children are taught to read Hebrew. These are the children who will soon be sent off to the gas chambers and the crematoria, and before them, they had been the children massacred in the long pogrom that is Jewish history. The teacher beseeches them:

> See my little ones, remember for all time
> What you are learning here
> When you, my dearest ones, in foreign exile dwell
> Wearied, brought low down,
> From these letters you will draw strength;
> Look into them.

|nobilmente| In the letters and words lives memory and hope, and they warm the soul as the body would be warmed before the hearth on a cold winter's night. In the written words, what is lost may be found. I write every day.

I have been considering that I organize much of my life attempting to deal with the inevitability of loss. In a sense, I set out to find things, and in the process of discovery I construct my life—in the hopeless hope that I can protect myself from the sense of inexorable loss or from having even to acknowledge its reality. I fill another journal, write another book, complete another photo album. But it is a futile endeavor for I have always missed some moment. Every moment lived is immediately lost and forever irrecoverable. I am immersed now in the joy of this moment, but it soon will be gone. And so I take this moment's photo now and place it conspicuously on the mantelpiece, or I paste it less obviously in a book. Sometimes I write it down. The moment is forever lost, but the memory, I hope, remains, though the memory remains suspect.

None of these choices is now available to my mother; she lives without this conflict and without the weight of memory.

I think that to hold on to such grief or joy is a burden I would prefer not to bear; the past might distract me from my life. It would color the present and is better forgotten and thus, lost. Perhaps this is what Emerson means in his essay "Experience" when he speaks specifically of his grief. He says, "So is it with this calamity; it does not touch me; something which I fancied was a part of me, which could not be torn away without tearing me nor enlarged without enriching me falls off from me and leaves no scar... I grieve that grief can teach me nothing, nor carry me one step into real nature." It is not that Emerson did not love his wife, his brother or his five-year old son, all of whom he has lost and for whom he grieved, but that his present life shows no trace of them. For Emerson, if there are no scars, then there was no rent, and no remnant of grief remains. Emerson remains whole; here, experience is not what he has had and upon which he reflects, but rather, experience is that in which he presently engages. The grief that has left no scar is not part of experience.

More than "Self-Reliance," more than the "American Scholar"—essays that every school child must read and believe—in "Experience," Emerson asserts the power of the individual to create her life absolutely, and he affirms his faith in the centrality of the present moment even in the face of insuperable loss or great joy. Emerson suggests that the grief he experienced as a result of the deaths of his wife, his brother and his dear five-year-old son, had not, in fact, touched him. Emerson argues that he is not diminished by these losses but remains whole and completely available still to experience. Ironically, I think, he writes himself to mental health. Though he avers that "intellectual tasting of life will not supersede muscular activity (an implied criticism of the Brook Farm experiment where "the noblest theory of life would not move a plough"), in fact, it is Emerson's intellect that saves him as he manages his grief. His narrative creates him. In it, he avows that there is nothing to be learned from his grief *nor* from his joy, I suspect, because they lead him nowhere. Outside the moment, nothing exists, though things like the deaths of this wife, brother and son can be brought into the moment and made into narrative. Emerson refers to that moment of creativity as 'power,' and that which is created in that moment, he calls 'form.' Emerson says, "These must be kept in some balance: a man is a golden impossibility. The line he must walk is a hair's breadth. The wise through excess of wisdom is made a fool." Isn't that exactly Hamlet's problem?

The native hue of resolution
Is sicklied o'er with the pale cast of thought,
And enterprises of great pitch and moment
With this regard their currents turn awry
And lose the name of action.

But, alas, *I* cannot act without thought, and then, the moment is lost. However, without form there is no life. It is Emerson's acknowledgement of the permanence of change, a synonym for loss, which inures him from its weight and ensures his absolute independence. The form moves into the future, but it has lost its meaning in the moment. Though Emerson is aware that everything must be eventually lost, his surety *of the next moment* enables him to go on even though this awareness is "the plaint of tragedy."

Nothing gold can stay, though in the moment it is gold. Acquisition in this world is endless and finally unsatisfying—else why the perpetual urge to acquire. Here, there is no end to the goods I can purchase; here, there is no limit to what I can obtain. But perhaps it is error to devote our lives to acquisition because whatever we acquire is eventually inevitably lost. Acquisition doesn't fulfill desire but only gives it a temporary outlet. And so we either continue to obtain and offer ourselves the illusion of permanence, or we must do something else to assuage or obscure our sense of loss. Even the words I write now are an attempt not to lose the moment and to somehow preserve it. The attempt is valiant but hopeless. The word remains, but the moment it attempts to preserve is gone. Thoughts fly up but the words remain below.

I think that is the problem that sent Thoreau out to Walden. He wanted to learn what was the least he needed to live so that he needn't spend his time acquiring that for which he had no need. Hence, his decision to discard the paper weight he had been given as a gift because he discovered that it accumulated dust to which he must attend. He had other priorities. All the wealth a person acquires doesn't actually raise the stature of a single person until s/he starts to actually 'lose' some of it, often in philanthropic activities. But of course, the wealthy have so much to begin with that the philanthropy has no consequence and is not in fact, actually a loss.

"Experience" is a complex essay, and when I read it, I am engaged in experience. When I think about the essay—even when I write about it—I engage in experience. The moment is soon lost, and I must step to the next. And I think that this is the very thin line that a human must walk. If I linger in memory, I lose the present; experience is not what we know in reflection but rather, what is now but is soon passed. Experience is too soon lost, and when I consider it or write about it, I give my life structure by the narrative, but the 'experience' of which I write is gone, though I am engaged in experience. It is impossible. Grief falls off me and does not touch me.

Ah, I wish it were so easy.

The sublime, I think, is the absolute immersion in the moment, and represents the opposite of loss, though it is finally irrecoverable as is the moment. It is, I believe, the sublime I would seek. Recently, the sublime came up in conversation with my daughter, who heard the term on a television show she was watching at the moment. She asked what the word meant. I told her that the sublime was an event that inspired an emotional response that filled her from her toes to her scalp but that was inexpressible, a feeling she might have experienced when she carried into our house her new eight-week-old kitten.

She nodded her head. After a moment's thought she asked, "Was the holocaust sublime?" It was a thoughtful question.

But I told her that in fact, I had always associated the sublime with more majestic heights. I said that I thought the sublime raised our lives to a deeper level of experience. Inexpressible as the holocaust may be, thoughts of it only drag me through the muck and the grime. However, I suggested to her, perhaps the response of the fighters in the Warsaw Ghetto and the courage with which they fought the Nazis might rise to the level of the sublime.

When I refer to the sublime, I refer to an event, physical or psychical, that inspires an emotional response that is essentially inarticulable (though I am going to try to articulate it here) and to which I attribute some state of transcendence. I experience the sublime though I cannot will it. To experience the sublime is to occupy completely my physical space and to feel for even a brief moment an emotional force rise up within me—not unlike a wave, I think—that pulls me up away from the quotidian and the ocean's rocky and shell-strewn floor, to stand divinely atop the world, like the man in the portrait long-associated with Byron's Manfred,. For example, sometimes I run in the early morning silences, and I have a sense that I am not alone though there is no one about me. I feel a presence. Dylan speaks of this particular experience in "Every Grain of Sand." He sings, "I hear the ancient footsteps, like the motion of the sea, Sometimes I turn there's someone there, other times it's only me." Dylan suggests to me that this perception is a mystical occurrence; at times we become receptive to a spiritual influx or presence, and we feel we are not alone. Perhaps this occurs when we are most free. I celebrate the times when there is someone there; but I think that I cannot plan those times, though I can leave myself open to them.

I cannot seek the sublime, but I recognize it when I experience it. For example this morning, it occurred as I listened to the first movement of Beethoven's Sixth Symphony. Like so many of my generation, I was first introduced to this music by Disney's *Fantasia* in which the animators choreographed the symphony in bucolic forest scenes with beautiful centaurs flirting, courting and innocently coupling. Even the fierce storm scene in the later movement is tamed by the playfully vindictive Zeus tossing lightning bolts down on the chubby Dionysius not sloppily drunk but swimming innocently happy in overflowing vats of wine. There is nothing in this performance except the mundane.

But toward the end of the first movement—almost at the very end, there occurs one of the most glorious melodies I have experienced. I cannot define the aggregate emotion I feel when I listen, but these measures pluck the strings of my soul as if the music were the wind and my soul the Aeolian Harp, and I experience absolute, uncorrupted and incorruptible joy. In it, I experience a sublime, transcendent moment. I feel complete, like a jig-saw puzzle into which the last piece has been placed, experience a yearning without emptiness and a desire without need. It is the emotion I felt in the birthing room when I first called my daughter by her name. I live in the world hoping to realize the sublime, to know that there is someone there. Sometimes, alas, it's only me. The sublime is in the world but not of the world, and properly, it should lead us changed back to the world.

I think I understand an expression of the sublime in Dan Bern's song, "God Said No." The piece as a whole is a bitter reflection on human hubris, vanity, incompetence and pettiness. In apparent earnestness, the speaker begs God to send him back in time so that his actions might alter history and prevent the tragedies we have experienced: the rise of Hitler, the suicide of Kurt Cobain, the death of Jesus. But God responds emphatically and says no, because though we humans espouse good intentions, we have not enough integrity and vision to accomplish much of anything. Rather than change history and save lives, we would become bogged down in selfish purposes and vague theory; we would change nothing. However, "God Said No" does offer a moment of insight—a transcendent and sublime moment: God says no because "Time, Time belongs to me /Time's my secret weapon /My final advantage." Time is not available to human influence. All we can affect by our actions is the present, but how our acts might change the future remains uncertain and even, unknown. And the speaker says, "God turned away/From the edge of town/I knew I was beaten/And that now was all I had." When God turns away from the edge of town, access to a past God can't (and won't) change is denied, and man is left to accomplish something in the present. And this fullness of understanding, this moment of the sublime, occurs where God must be met: on the edge of town: "Where the wind meets the stillness /Where the darkness meets the light /Where the ocean meets the sky /Where the desert meets the rain/Where the earth meets the heavens." On the edge of town there is nothing except promise.

I am reminded of Springsteen's 1978 paean to that same darkness at the edge of town and the moment of the sublime that he celebrates:

I'll be on that hill with everything I got
Lives on the line where dreams are found and lost
I'll be there on time and I'll pay the cost
For wanting things that can only be found
In the darkness on the edge of town

In Springsteen's world, that darkness at the edge of town is where one confronts and realizes one's hopes and dreams. No wonder it is a place where no one looks too long in your face. Thoreau said that he never met a person fully awake, and wondered how he would ever be able to look anyone in the face. Moses must wear a mask during his life for his face is terrifyingly aglow with the present. For Dan Bern, that darkness is where God leaves humanity to itself, and for Springsteen the darkness at the edge of town is the moment of the transcendence. It is as if to be in the darkness at the edge of town is the only and worst place to be. The darkness at the edge of town is where the sublime can be experienced. Jacob, having run away from his home after having deceived his father and brother, must have been on the edge of town when he stopped for the night on his way to Haran. "Taking one of the stones of that place, he put it under his head and lay down in that place. He had a dream." It is in that dream that God speaks to Jacob and promises him land, prosperity and power. God assures Jacob that God "will not leave you until I have done what I have promised you." I think that this must have been an awesome dream, and Jacob awakens from it and says, "Surely the Lord is present in this place, and I, I did not know it." It is the experience of the sublime; it occurs in the moment and then is gone. There was nothing there except the dream.

I've learned to seek the darkness at the edge of town, and I would be on time whenever that might be.

/*animato*/ At the bottom of the paved, sloped driveway, I stopped the car and got out to gather up my mail. I live in another country, so to speak, and the post office vehicle must drive along the side of the frontage road delivering the mail to roadside boxes. I rarely see the postal carrier, but she must know something *about* me from the mail she deposits *for* me.

As I said, I stopped to pick up the mail, and today, there was nothing except shopping catalogs that I did not request and campaign literature from candidates for whom I will not vote in the upcoming election, and, of course, some bills. Everybody wants either my financial or electoral support, and they seem determined that I wear their clothes or purchase their products. There is never anything in the mail that holds very much interest to me, but I religiously attend to the daily ritual of retrieving it. When I was growing up, I assiduously watched on the family television as Michael Anthony handed out tax-free checks for one million dollars to carefully chosen individuals offering them an opportunity to start life anew. The dramatic interest of the show, "The Millionaire," consisted in how the money would alter the lives of those for whom the gift of that money had such potential, though often the change occurred in ways no one would have anticipated. "Let's see how this will make a difference," Tipton would say to Michael Anthony, handing him the tax-free cashier's check for $1,000,000 that he was to deliver to the next millionaire. I always thought that *my* family could have used that million dollars. When I was older, I read *King Lear* and I understood better the show's premise. "As flies to wanton boys are we to th' gods, They kill us for their sport," says Gloucester. Playthings all. There was nothing there except disappointment.

I was imprinted by this television show nonetheless (as by not a few others as well; I have barely been able to overcome the influence of some of them), and though my doorbell has not functioned in year, and though I do not think Michael Anthony still serves John Beresford Tipton, I open my mailbox every day hoping to discover I have been chosen as the newest plaything of the gods. It is a silly anticipation, really. Perhaps it is the enactment of Desire—I don't know what I am waiting for or from whom I await some communication. And I must admit that I can't really imagine how the money or the arrival of anything much might change my life. I have developed only those needs for which my academic salary has permitted me, and for a long time, I have studied and admired Henry David Thoreau. He admonishes me to be happy within my means; he maintained no mailbox at Walden. I receive too much mail. But today as I have said, there was nothing in the mailbox except shopping catalogs that I did not request and campaign literature from some candidates for whom I will not vote, and my bills, minimal though they be now. I will pay them in good time.

I've lived virtually alone since my divorce ten years ago and have been retired now for the past six years. My mailbox remains some connection to an outside world, though the tie from today's mail is a tenuous one. The children are quite far-flung, and most communication with them occurs through cell phone calls, texts, and emails. From these sources, I receive my share of chatter, and even sometimes, words of consequence. I include them—the children and the words—in my work. There is no one living in my house except me.

Every day now, I fill the same mug with brewed coffee, and walk to the cabin office behind my house where I do some work. It is now a casual endeavor. After forty-two years in the classroom, I retired to create and enter an occasional virtual class. On most days, I sit before the computer screen and follow the conversations I have organized, I read and comment on papers I have assigned, and occasionally post a comment that has provoked some thought of mine. I have learned from these virtual experiences that when offered the appropriate environment, students will ask and answer most of the questions I once thought part of my purview. In my present incarnation, my virtual invisibility has become essential to education. Nothing usually enters my solitude except the wind outside of my windows.

Today, I throw the mail onto the floor of the passenger side of my car. Today, I am not going into the office. When I return home I will transfer the pile to the recycling bins. There is nothing left to do now except go.

I head the car out to the road through town that will take me to the interstate highway. I have a considerable drive ahead of me. In New York City, where I lived for fifteen years, one measures distance in time, but out here in the mid-west, distance is measured in miles: in the same amount of time one can travel sixty miles in the mid-west or 60 blocks in New York City. Traveling is a wholly different experience in each place. Today I am heading the sixty miles into Minneapolis. A friend's daughter has had a child, and I am going to his *brit*. One doesn't get invited to a brit; one just arrives.

Having had two daughters, I did not have to celebrate a *brit milah* for them. I did not know the sex of the first child before her birth, but I do my concern that should the child turn out to have a penis, I would have to make a decision on what if anything should happen to it. Though every male I have known and seen naked was circumcised, most ritualistically at *brit milahs* and some according to fashion by doctors in the hospital, I developed countercultural motives to avoid this procedure, though I think it was my own squeamishness and trepidation that influenced me the most. I wondered how—and certainly why—I would or even could ever with intent physically hurt an eight day old infant, cut and remove a piece of his flesh and leave him irremediably altered. I was concerned about the letting of blood from my first-born child for a procedure of no medical value and of dubious rationale. But I also worried how the failure to hold a *brit milah* would affect my own and my wife's parents, and how it might later cause some consternation to the child himself when in the shower he would note that he didn't look like me there. And then there was tradition and behind that, history. But our first-born was a girl and the issue was resolved naturally. For the second child there was no concern. Though I had asked not to be informed of the sex of the child, I became aware that none of the clothes from the older daughter had been passed on. There was nothing to expect except a girl.

The second time that God establishes a covenant with Abraham, God demands that Abraham participate in the promise. "This is my covenant which you are to keep, between me and you and your seed after you: every male among you shall be circumcised. You shall circumcise the flesh of your foreskin, so that it may serve as a sign of the covenant between me and you. At eight days old, every male among you shall be circumcised, throughout your genera-tions . . . so that my covenant may be in your flesh as a covenant for the ages." And immediately, as was his wont, Abraham acceded to God's command. Taking all of the men of his household, his thirteen-year-old son, Ishmael, and himself, he circumcised each. Just before God's command concerning circumcision, he changes Abram's name to Abraham and Sarai's name to Sarah, adding the letter '*hay*' to both of their names to indicate their association with God.

Brit milah serves as the entrance for the male child into the Jewish community. The practice literally marks the covenant in the flesh of the male child. Opponents to circumcision say the procedure is cruel, akin to cliteroidectomy and other barbaric mutilating practices engaged in by native tribes and roundly criticized by the civilized world. Apparently about forty or fifty years ago, almost 90% of all boys received circumcision, many, of course, in hospital because they weren't Jewish. It was then, for whatever reason, considered a stylish and proper procedure. Today it is no longer believed to be so, and I read that fewer than 60% of males receive circumcision. It is no longer fashionable.

Of late I find this argument against circumcision unconvincing. I think that we cut our flesh and that of our children all of the time. For example, many of our young people these days pierce their ears, and often do so several times. Ear cartilages are regularly punctured through. My own two children have marked a path up their ear lobes; my dearest friend's daughter pierced her navel interrupting, my friend moans (with rings dangling from her own ears), an important chakra path. Indeed, the bodies of so many have been pierced in many places, some of which I prefer not to consider; the penises of some males, and the navels, nipples and clitorises of some women being popular sites. Hamlet asks, who would such fardels bear when one could her quietus make with a bare bodkin? And I look about and people are pricking themselves with these bodkins with some frequency, and I do not hear much public outcry condemning such practice. Some would say that these are voluntary acts by mature adults, but the jewelry that adorns the faces and bodies of many of our children, some still under the age of one, belies this argument.

Tattoos are visible on many citizens who might once have eschewed company with anyone sporting such bodily attire. Personally, I experience these tattoos as a form of violence. They remind me at times of the t-shirts I hate to stare at but which demand that I do so—like the ones which have blazoned across the chest, "Do not stare at my chest." These tattoos demand to be seen, and though I need not look, why else are they so obviously visible? Many of the designs are somewhat simple, and some, I think, even inconspicuously placed; some, I am certain, I never see at all, though I suspect they serve some purpose about which I would prefer not to know. However, the ones I do see—and they are ubiquitous today—even people of my generation carry them as marks upon the flesh—are very much in view on arms, legs, on chests, and on the smalls and larges of backs, on shoulders left and right, and on heads and necks. And then there are elaborately designed tattoos that cover entire body parts and are inked in strong, bold patterns and colors, leaving no skin unmarked, and I feel assaulted by the broadcast volume and the demand to view. Just yesterday, I saw a tattoo encircling the left ankle—almost like a bracelet. Not at all delicate, it was inked in black and appeared to me drawn in the image of barbed wire. As a society we are tolerant of these practices and intolerant of circumcision.

I've gotten older, and I've grown, if not more comfortable to the actual moment of the *brit milah*, at least more prepared to respond to the accusation that circumcision is a barbaric rite. For me, the *brit milah* contains and celebrates thousands of years of history, struggle and survival in the face of insurmountable odds and unconscionable violence. It is a minor pin-prick in the entire life of the child, but it joins him viscerally and irrevocably to the community and to a history that can be dismissed only at significant cost. Inherently, sexism is implicit in the ceremony, and I read that feminists propose several practices that might serve as a female counterpart to the *brit milah*: washing the soles of the feet of the eight day old girl, or the breaking of the hymen. I do not know what I think of these ideas, but for me, the practice of *brit milah* retains yet the cultish aspects of a Judaism that rose up out of an almost universal barbarism and that preached care for the widow, the orphan and the stranger in our midst. It is important to recognize the history undergirding our actions and sometimes to align our actions to honor and to sustain that history into the present.

/*expressivo*/ Something has brought me to the present, but all that has done so I will never know. Nonetheless, my presence here is incontrovertible. Marx said that everyone makes her own history, but they do not make it as they please. I am inclined to accept his observation. That is, we do not choose the circumstances in which our choices are made though we must always accept the consequences of our choices. I daily confront and act upon those circumstances that derive inevitably from my semi-obscured pasts. I married for love and divorced in rancor. What didn't I know and why? I did not choose my family of origin or the circumstances in which I was raised. My parents might have chosen to have children, but did they expect me? Was I some fulfillment of their expectations for life, and have I been successful in fulfilling them? What were my choices? Not all of the candidates for whom I voted have been elected to office, and my will was thwarted as a result.

I act from an interminable number of decisions I make each day, though often, I think, I am not consciously aware that I have actually made a decision. In circumstances I have not wholly constructed, I act, and though I have learned to assume responsibility, indeed, sometimes even take pride in that assumption, I also recognize that such pride derives from a very limited perspective. I acknowledge readily and regretfully—or is this admission just an excuse for the many errors I have made—that to ascribe any sense of complete knowledge is a fiction. Marx said that the traditions of all past dead generations weigh like a nightmare on the brain. Stephen Daedulus says that history is a nightmare from which he is attempting to awaken, and my dearest friend describes the present as a nightmare. What might be so frightening about nightmares is that in them I lack any semblance of control over my behavior; in my nightmares I am always threatened with dissolution. Perhaps nightmares develop from the fear of lack of control that the nightmares enact. Last night I dreamed that every time I stood up to assert my presence there was already someone standing in my place. In my nightmare, I was reduced to silence and helplessness. My nightmares arise out of my greatest fear: that I am out of control. But perhaps the whole belief that I am ever in control is the fiction. When Montaigne says that "I find myself more by chance encounter than by searching my judgment" I think I know what he means. I live a great deal in illusion.

My current situation is the result of a history of which I am not fully aware, and over which certainly I have had only marginal control. I go to therapy to narrate that history and ascribe to it causality. In my sessions, I offer up my history by writing a past, inscribing myself in that history. It is a nice fiction. Though actively imagining a past, it is really the future with which I am concerned. I require a particular past so I can change direction from it. I need a past so that I can keep on keeping on. Perhaps it is all a fiction. Even my changes are partly a result of conditions not of my choosing. If they change the rules, then I either subscribe to the variation or suffer the consequences. There are almost always pieces of the puzzle missing, and I don't even know what the picture is supposed to look like. When I was just a little girl, I asked my mother what would I be, and she answered, what will be will be. *Qué sera, sera.* Perhaps the sublime is a respite from history though what brings me to the sublime moment is always history.

≈

A sublime digression:
/*energico*/ In a rather lengthy and complicated discussion, the Rabbis argue that when both parties cannot agree on a division of property, a division can be made only if after the division each part will retain the designation applied to the whole. That is, a division that reduces a courtyard to less than four cubits—the minimum size ascribed to a courtyard—shall not be made. Many complications and serious digressions arise in the course of this discussion

Now, because the Rabbis are always concerned with a great deal more than the topic of their discussion, because always underlying their discussion is the ethics that comprise a moral and holy life, the conversation concerning a division of property leads eventually to a discussion of the division and separation of any number of disparate items, one of those items being the division of scriptural scrolls.

After all, the entire scripture—the Five Books of Moses, the Prophets and the Hagiographia—is lengthy and a single scroll would end up rather heavy. If one does not mind this weight, then it is permissible to fasten them all together, given a few spatial stipulations, but the Rabbis say, that if a man wants to divide the Law, the Prophets and the Hagiographia he may do so, given a few restrictions. And one rule concerns the size of the Torah Scroll.

The Rabbis argue that the size of a scroll of the Law—Torah— should be such that its length does not exceed its circumference and that its circumference does not exceed its height. Which is all well and good, I suppose, but this does not answer for the actual *size* of the scroll. Rabbi (Judah Ha-Nasi) taught that using thick parchment the scroll should be six handbreadths, though using thin parchment the size would be indeterminate. Who knows how thin parchment could be made! Now, a handsbreadth—about three inches—is equal to four fingerbreadths, and a cubit is equal to six handbreadths. Thus, a cubit, originally the length of a man's arm from the elbow to the tip of the middle finger, is equal to about eighteen inches. According to Judah Ha-Levi, a Torah Scroll with thick parchment might be approximately eighteen inches in height and circumference! However, an objection was raised to this measurement:

It is written that the ark Moses carried in the wilderness was 2½ cubits long (forty-five inches), 1½ cubits wide (twenty-seven inches) , and 1½ cubits in height. Into the ark were placed the tablets on which Moses had carved the Ten Commandments. Those tablets were said to be six hands breadth, or one cubit each in length and therefore, took up twelve hands breadth, or two cubits, in the ark, leaving three hands breadth space left. Assuming another hands breadth was taken up by the thickness of the wood, then two hands breadth space remained in the ark. The Rabbis cannot imagine, I think, that Moses would build an ark and leave empty space. Nor can the Rabbis imagine that God would command the building of an ark with extraneous space. As there is not supposed to be a superfluous or unnecessary word in Scriptures, there ought not to be in the ark an extraneous fingerbreadth in measurement. In the ark there should not be any empty space. Thus, the Rabbis say that into the ark must have been placed the Torah scroll, and it could have been only two hands breadth in size. It is taught that "Moses received the Torah from Sinai and transmitted it to Joshua; Joshua to the Elders; the Elders to the Prophets; and the Prophets transmitted it to the Men of the Great Assembly." The Torah that we read and study is the original work. It exists and has always done so. But, in fact, there is no explicit mention of the Torah's presence in the Ark. Not a word. Anywhere.

And since there is no mention of this presence anywhere in all of Scripture, the Rabbis have to invent such mention. And they do so by going to *II Chronicles* 5:10 which reads, "There was nothing in the ark save the two tables of stone which Moses put there." Now, it would seem quite clear from this sentence that there was nothing in the ark but the two tablets onto which Moses had carved the Ten Commandments, but the Rabbis argue that this is not so at all. They say, "Now in the words '*nothing*' and '*save*' we have a limitation following a limitation, and the purpose of a limitation following a limitation is to intimate the presence of something which is not mentioned." Sublime.

This is a hermeneutical device about which I have never heard, nor could ever imagine, I think. Two absences that intimate a presence. How do the Rabbis create a presence out of two absences? Let me try this: it is clear to the Rabbis that the Torah contains not a single extra word. If *II Chronicles* wanted to indicate the contents of the ark it need have said that "Only the tablets were in the ark," and would not have required the construction 'nothing . . . except.' The use of both words, however, suggests that there is more to be understood. Thus, the Rabbis reason, two absences suggest a presence. I have seen enough crime shows on the television: "What did you say to the victim the last time you saw her?"

"Nothing."

"Nothing at all?"

And here the one being questioned says either "Nothing," in which case the interview is over, or, "Nothing except . . ." in which case the two limitations intimate the presence of something else!!

How prescient the Rabbis were. How well they understood human psychology.

But the question remains: *why* did the Rabbis invent this rule?? And I am going to suggest that it has something to do with history. *Pirke Avot* begins, "Moses received the Torah from Sinai and transmitted it to Joshua; Joshua to the Elders; the Elders to the Prophets; and the Prophets transmitted it to the Men of the Great Assembly." *Deuteronomy* 17:18 commands that when the people choose a king and he is seated on his throne that a copy of "this Teaching" be written for him on a scroll by the levitical priests." There is no indication in what form "this Teaching" existed and from whence its origin. Other than this statement, or the Rabbinic account of the transmission of Torah, except in *Devarim*, when Moses urged the people to live by the words of God that are found in the Book of the Torah, and in 31:9 when it is said that "Moses wrote this Torah and gave it to the Kohanim, the sons of Levi, the bearers of the Ark of the covenant of God, and to all the elders of Israel," there is no mention anywhere of the actual physical presence of a Torah Scroll. There is some vague reference in *Exodus* that after God writes the Ten Commandments on the second set of tablets, Moses writes down the "other" commandments, "for in accordance with these commandments I make a covenant with you and with Israel." Of course, these *commandments* are found in the last three books of the Torah, but the origin for the first two books must still be accounted. In between verse 1 and verse 27 God delivers to Moses a series of commandments that the people must follow, but it is forty days and night that Moses stays atop the mountain. He must have written quite a bit, in fact. The Rabbis ascribe the Torah to Moses' effort. But, if the Rabbis cannot locate Torah at Revelation, then the sacred nature of Holy Scripture has been lost, and Revelation becomes another foolhardy play for power. If it becomes clear that Torah did not derive from Sinai, then its authority is diminished. History demands the presence of Torah at Sinai, and so the Rabbis must situate it there in history. Of course, as narrative this history is a fiction, but it is a very useful fiction. Justice, justice thou shalt pursue!

/animato/ We stand about, as if we have been posed by a painter hired to immortalize the scene, arranged in small groups engaged in various animated appearances of intimacies; actually we are making talk smaller and awaiting the arrival of the really significant player in this drama. I suppose that I might refer to the child as the 'actor' but in fact there is nothing except his presence and his foreskin required. He is at the moment peacefully asleep in his bedroom on the other side of the house. The twenty or so guests are gathered in the living room of the child's parents. Nothing moves except the lips of the one in a group speaking.

The room itself is small and rectangular with a large fireplace against the North wall. Despite the frigid weather, no fire has been built. Across from the fireplace and parallel to it on the shorter sides of the rectangle are four uncovered, oversized windows that looked out over a wooded area in which room, I have been told, deer and an occasional fox. Snow covers the ground and the trees stand vulnerably naked. The walls are painted a pale yellow that suffuses the room with a quiet calm. Paintings and photos sacred to the family cover the mantel piece. Standing together near the window are the child's father and the father's father; both are draped in full-length talleisim that they have drawn up and hung over their shoulders. They stand with their backs to the room looking out of the windows toward the woods. The father puts his arm about his son and speaks something quietly, even conspiratorially in his ear. If I were either of these men I would be tense, but whatever it was they said it provoked laughter in both of them. They return to gazing silently out of the windows.

To the right of both men and apart from them stands the mohel, the man responsible for performing the circumcision. He is a fairly young man, probably in his late thirties. His beard is dark and well trimmed. He wears a black suit and a red and yellow striped tie. He, too, wears a full length tallit. He does not seem part of the gathering though he is very much engaged in the process. As he stands over his waist-high table and professionally moves about ensuring himself that everything he needs is ready and at hand, his tallit sways as if blown by some wind. His busy-ness makes him stand out in the crowded room, and it seems to me as if he is the only truly self-animated body in this congregation. He sings a bit to himself while he prepares. To the left of the table is a large upholstered velvet Queen Anne chair, and on that chair is an oversized bed pillow covered with a fresh white case. On the other side of the table is a matching Queen Anne chair on which no pillow had been placed.

As if the director has called for action, the room becomes animated. The small groups dissolve, transforming into twenty individuals. The baby has been asleep in his own room, but when he is carried into the room cradled in his mother's mother's arms, he is awake though perhaps, not aware. Better for him I think. It is considered an honor to be asked to carry the eight-day-old child into the room for his *brit*, and this grandmother smiles broadly as she enters with her grandson. Not that much older than myself, she is rather attractive. Her graying hair is carefully styled and cropped close to her head. As she walks into the room, she stares down at the child swaddled and barely visible amidst the bundle of wrappings, and this *bubbe* smiles deeply. Everyone turns towards the entryway and as is customary at this moment, calls out *Baruch Haba*. "Blessed is he who comes."

This declaration (I am not certain that it is indeed, a blessing) initiates the ceremony of the *brit milah*. It seems to me a rather interesting linguistic construction. The action implied by the verb is in fact not accurate to the infant for whose *brit milah* we have all gathered. Rather, the child has been carried into this place by his terribly proud grandmother. At the moment, he is passive, unaware and quite help-less. I think it is a lovely practice to greet the newborn child with such language of approval. More than a simple acknowledgement of presence, the word 'blessed' refers both to the child who is blessed and to we who can bless and have come to join in this ceremony. The latter refers to the responsibility we accept by bringing the child into the community with this *brit milah*; the former refers to the child who is now to become a member. Within the language is embedded some glorious hope that *this* child might be the blessed Messiah for whom Jews wait, while the significance of this child is reinforced by the language's formality acknowledging his arrival and blessedness. I suppose it has become a cliché to say that the birth of every child promises the world the hope of redemption, but the language here seems addressed pointedly to the arrival of someone very special and whose arrival seems purposed and purposeful. There was nothing in the language except hope and joy.

At the end of our Passover Seders we celebrants join in incantatory song: *l'shanah haba, b'yerushalim*, a phrase that seems to be generally translated as "next year in Jerusalem." Literally the words mean *to the year that is coming in Jerusalem* and that by implication is not present here. But at this *brit milah* and with the entrance of this child the phrase *baruch haba*, speaks to the child's presence and to the forth-coming circumcision. This act will bring the child into the covenant made between God and Abraham—albeit, we must admit, without the child's consent or even knowledge—and in the verb rests pres-ent and future, again a reference to the arrival of the Messiah. It is rumored that the Messiah is already in our midst and awaits the right moment to reveal himself. Blessed is he who comes.

The child is carried to the Queen Anne wing chair to the left of the surgical table and placed gently on the pillow. For the purpose of this *brit milah*, this chair has been designated as Elijah's chair. Since Elijah is traditionally recognized as the forerunner of the Messiah, Elijah is invited to every *brit milah*: every newborn child could be the Messiah, and clearly, Elijah needs to know him. As the grandmother places the child on the pillow, the mohel intones in Hebrew, "This is the throne of Elijah the prophet, may he be remembered for good." Interestingly, there is no responsive Amen. The words are not so much a prayer, as a directive. That I suppose might still necessitate a response of amen, but we remain silent. There is nothing to do but silently accept the directive. The mohel reaches down and gently lifts the child to the table where the *brit* will be performed. The pacific murmuring of the child is the only sound in the room.

The Rabbis tell us that the human came into being as the final creation so that it might never be presumed that God had an accomplice in creation. In the beginning of God's creation, no other consciousness exists outside that of God and God's messengers, or angels as they are commonly called. And as there are stories of the angels offering advice to God regarding creation, so might it be assumed that had they been present, conscious humans might have offered a few suggestions of their own in the process. But the Rabbis declare that as the last element to be created, the human, could claim to have had any part in the preceding handiwork. Indeed, the world is a magnificent accomplishment, and the Rabbis are insistent that humans take no credit for its presence. It is only on the sixth day, with the creation of human being and the inhabitation of the Garden, that God refers to God's work as 'very' good. Only with the presence of the human being is God's creation complete, and so humans cannot be considered partners in the work. Blessed be he who comes.

Alternatively, another Rabbi has suggested that humans were created on the last day of creation so that they might always be reminded that the gnat was created prior. This explanation serves as an absolute check on human pride, but despite repeated evidence to the contrary, human pride has never taken the explanation seriously. As the father of the atomic bomb J. Robert Oppenheimer famously quoted from the Bhagavad Gita, "Now I am become death, the destroyer of worlds."

I worry about the world my children—this child here—will be left to inherit.

I wonder why the presence of 'gnats,' and mosquitoes, and diseases and horrible disfigurements are necessary at all. I know, I know, that this is Job's question, and I know God's answer: who are you to wonder? But before the arrival of the human being in the Garden, all of these afflictions remained unbothersome, unconscious, unnamed and in the absence of human beings, without menace.

I do not know where the sublime may be found; I experience it in odd moments and unexpected events. When my mother moved from her home to an assisted living arrangement, she mailed me her papers. That day, there was nothing in my mailbox except this large manila envelope filled with a seemingly random assortment of memorabilia: a newspaper clipping announcing the unusual multiple birth of a brood of Shetland sheepdogs, one of which we purchased; some letters I had written home from college (terribly embarrassing to read now); a few old photographs, some even of me; and a eulogy for Abel Hirsh, my grandfather's brother whom I had never met and of whom I had no information. There was nothing about my mother in there except my letters to her.

The paper on which the eulogy was typed had yellowed over the years and was somewhat brittle. Unlike the crisply smooth white paper on which contemporary computer printers print, this paper was thick and though not rough, it certainly also was not smooth. The eulogy had been flawlessly typed on a typewriter, but in intentional blank spaces a handwritten Hebrew text had been inserted. No vowel markings existed except under a single word. I don't know enough Hebrew to understand why only this word is vocalized. Hebrew is a consonantal language and is usually written without vowels; there is nothing in the text except the consonants. Sometimes this creates problems for comprehension and sometimes this limitation offers remarkable opportunities for interpretation. Rabbi Drob needed none. He began: "In every Rabbi's archives may be found a number of sermons that for some reason or other were never completed. Like the finished sermons, they were thoroughly planned in the mind even before they were set to paper, and when the writing began, they seemed destined for delivery in the pulpit. A beautiful introduction was written, the proposition was clearly stated and the main argument definitely advanced. But then something happened, (even the Rabbi does not recall it now) which caused another sermon to be substituted for it. The manuscript was laid aside for some other occasion, and there it reposes, an abortive effort, some day to be completed and given its chance in the pulpit." These beautiful opening phrases were spoken at the funeral of my grandfather's brother, a Rabbi, who died in 1935 at the age of fifty-one, a victim of the encephalitis lethargica epidemic that plagued the United States from 1917-1927. Encephalitis lethargica is a sleeping sickness, though not *the* sleeping sickness. In about 1919, Abel must have suffered from a somewhat severe sore throat, and then rather rapidly slipped into a sleep from which he could be aroused only occasionally. He was not in a coma—there was significant brain activity—and he could even at times open his eyes and speak. Abel's brother, my grandfather, my mother's father, arrived every day at the hospital to feed Abel.

But for the most part of sixteen years, he remained asleep in a bed at Montefiore Hospital in New York. If he dreamt, there is no record.

Abel Hirsh (neé Hirschowitz) had been a student of Talmud at the Slabodka Yeshiva in Lithuania. This school was one of the premier Jewish learning institutions in Eastern Europe. Apparently, Abel was an unusually brilliant student, and he soon began to surpass his teachers in learning. He traveled to Frankfurt-am-Main, but soon discovered that there was no future for a Jew in Germany—how prescient his thought was at the time. He emigrated to the United States. A year after receiving his Masters Degree in Philosophy from Columbia University, he received his rabbinic ordination in 1908 from the Jewish Theological Seminary—it is said that his genius dazzled even the great Dr. Schechter—and all delighted in his conversation and his joy. He became a pulpit Rabbi.

But apparently, Rabbi Abel did not find much satisfaction in the profession: Rabbi Drob, who must have known Abel well, remarked sadly, "Too soon he discovered that in this land a glib tongue and a sonorous voice are valued far above deep scholarship and genuine piety. He was heartbroken over this disregard of scholarship and he could not bring himself to perform the tasks of a pulpit entertainer and social mixer which are so often demanded of the rabbi." Abel was one of the early graduates of the Jewish Theological Seminary as it became the center of the newly developing Conservative movement in Judaism under the leadership of Solomon Schechter. It was at Schechter's Jewish Theological Seminary that the Conservative Rabbis who would occupy the synagogue pulpits in the United States were educated and ordained.

Theirs was not an easy calling. Between 1912 and 1918, Abel Hirsh was employed as Rabbi in Huntsville, Alabama; Tucson, Arizona; Selma, Alabama; and East St. Louis, Illinois. He may have had some association with a congregation in Woonsocket, Rhode Island and Loraine, Ohio. His tenure at any one of these locations did not last more than two years. I do not think he enjoyed his work. Indeed, an historian at the Jewish Theological Seminary writes that "these first Conservative rabbis express frustration with the philistine congregants and uncouth board members, such as the synagogue president who 'wipes his nose with a tablecloth . . . and keeps his shop open on the Sabbath'. . . . [these Rabbis] confide unhappiness over their thwarted ambitions and painful isolation, living as they did in the cultural backwaters of America." But what nearly all of his students found in the field was less than encouraging. Most of Schechter's students moved from one congregation to the next, earning meager salaries, and for the most part, unable to implement any sort of successful program. Their lives were unfinished sermons.

I resonate with the situation in which Rabbi Abel and his colleagues found themselves. For forty years, I have been a teacher in the public schools, and I have wandered in the wilderness heartbroken over the disregard for scholarship and rigor that has come to characterize the American schools and that derives in large part from the utilitarianism that has come to dominate school learning, the economic austerity to which the schools have been forever subject, and the self-serving intrigues of our politicians who scapegoat the educational system—and especially the teachers—so as to obscure their own dissembling and pusillanimity. They fool me to the top of my bent.

For Abel, there was nothing in the Rabbinic calling except disappointment. Aspiring to serve both God and the congregation, Abel experienced only frustration and failure. He could not complete what he set out to accomplish. In the minutes of Mishkan Israel the following was recorded for March 16, 1918:

> At a special meeting of the Board of Trustees of Congregation Mishkan Israel held on Monday evening March 16th, the following resolutions were unamously [sic] adopted:
>
> "Whereas our Rabbi Dr. Abel Hirsch [sic] during a discourse on Friday evening March 13th at the Temple during the Sabbath services used and embraced language which not only was rude and considered out of place, but mortifying and insulting to the members of our congregation.
>
> "Be it further resolved, that we consider such utterances on the part of a Jewish Rabbi unjustifiable, degrading and demoralizing, and herewith express our indignation at such conduct.
>
> "That it is the sentiment of this Board that discourses of a like nature will not be tolerated in the future.
>
> "Be it further resolved that a copy of these resolutions be transmitted to our Rabbi Dr. Abel Hirsch [sic], and that he be asked to appear before present Board of Trustees on Wednesday evening at 8 o'clock at the Harmony club.
>
> – L. Thalheimer, Sec

I wonder what it was that Rabbi Hirsch might have said to so upset his congregation. But apparently Rabbi Hirsch appeared before the

Board of Trustees on the date required, and the following was subsequently entered into the Temple minutes:

March 18, 1914

On March 18th the Meeting was called to order at 8:00 PM at the Harmony Club M.J. Meyer presided.

"The following Members were present: J. Rothschild, B.J. Schuster, Mr. Rothenberg, et al.

"Dr. Hirsch [sic] appeared before the Meeting as requested and the President stated that his last discourse on Friday night has been insulting to every member of the Congregation and that he would like to have a statement from him and an explanation.

"The Rabbi stated that his remarks were not intended to be insulting to anybody, but they were misinterpreted and he was admonished to change his methods of conducting the Sunday School and confine his lectures to religious subjects only.

"The Meeting was a very harmonious one and satisfactory to the Rabbi,
as well as the Board.

– L. Thalheimer, Sec"

I am not fooled by Secretary Thalheimer's seemingly final conciliatory comment for on March 18 in a hand written letter, Rabbi Abel Hirsch resigned his pulpit at Mishkan Israel. *Mishkan* in Hebrew means tabernacle. There was nothing in the tabernacle except the tablets.

Rabbi Drob's eulogy says that Abel's body, 'weakened by this spiritual anguish,' finally succumbed to the dread 'sleeping sickness,' in which he had lain for *sixteen years* a living corpse doomed to a 'mattress grave.' From the beginning of his sickness in late 1918 or early 1919 until his death on Purim, 1935, Abel did not rise from his bed. Rabbi Drob acknowledges, "In God's archives, too, may be found many unfinished sermons, lives that began so beautifully, that were prepared so thoroughly for their God given tasks, and yet their fragrant flowers did not mature into the ripe fruit." So was it for Abel, I think. I ache for his disenchantment. I have become a scholar and am sorely disaffected by the social critique to which educators are subject, and the remarkably anti-intellectual and uncivil nature of contemporary society. Like so many a beautiful life that is destined to "blush unseen, an unfinished symphony, a painful earnest of what might have been," Abel died in 1935, his spirit crushed and his mind paralyzed by sleep. Over the years, this eulogy breaks my heart.

I am named for Abel. The 'A' of my name was meant to honor his life. There is nothing in my relationship to Abel except the sublime.

/*cantabile*/ The grandfather father lifts the child from Elijah's seat, and with the baby in his arms, walks to the chair on the other side of the table on which lies a clamp, a scalpel and some gauze, a bottle of wine and a cup, and sits down in the chair with the child in his lap. I knew that in the more Orthodox ceremonies the godfather holds the child in his lap for the circumcision, but this mohel and this family had opted for the more steady table on top of which was placed a plastic board with some restraining straps, and so this act of the *sandek* sitting with the infant is a symbolic one. The mohel recites the appropriate prayer: "Blessed are You, Lord our God, Ruler of the Universe, who has made us holy through his commandments, and has commanded us concerning circumcision." It crosses my mind that it is not the commandments that make us holy but our obedience to them from which our holiness derives. Human actions sanctify our lives. The *brit milah* is the choice of action here.

The mohel reaches down, raises the child up from his grandfather's lap, and places him professionally and gently on the table. The family and friends of the parents form a rather irregular and somewhat crowded semi-circle. The child's mother stays in the rear, and turns from the table on which lies her son. The boy's father, wrapped in his tallit stands attentively, though a bit uncertainly, to the mohel's left. I place myself toward the back, still a bit squeamish and by nature, withdrawn.

At first, the mohel gently unsnaps the bottom of the child's one-sies and unfastens each side of the disposable diaper, professionally and delicately pulling it out from under the child. Then, he recites the prayer: *"Behold, I am prepared and ready to perform the positive commandment that God has commanded us, to circumcise."* I like that every action is preceded by a blessing. It raises events out of the technical and the mundane onto some spiritual plane. I remember reading once that it is possible to transform even the most common event into one with extraordinary dimensions by simply adding the work *ta-keh* to the sentence. *Ta-keh* is a Yiddish word that interrupts the flow of the sentence and directs attention to the words following. Thus, instead of saying "Ah, there is a tree," I would say, "Ah, there is *ta-keh* a tree," the insertion of the word transforming the event into something remarkable, even miraculous. A blessing serves the same function. *Blessed are you, God, for having commanded us on the rite of circumcision,"* the mohel says, never taking his gaze from the child! From where I stand, I can see movement and hear the clicking of instruments—I am surprised to hear, *ta-keh*, a *nigun* being sung by the mohel—but for the most part, he remains hunched over the baby. At first, the baby burbles. Soon and quite professionally, the mohel performs the clamping of the foreskin and then the cutting; the baby cries out sharply and everyone, except perhaps the mohel whose *nigun* increases a bit in volume, ceases to breathe. The baby's mother's eyes are shut tightly and her bottom lip has turned a sharp red where her front teeth have bitten into it. Her own mother has her arm about her daughter's waist, and though the grandmother stares straight ahead, she is short enough not to have a view of the actual procedure. The child's father and grandfather stand silently, side-by-side, but untouching, each wrapped in his tallit and private thoughts. The child continues to scream, but the mohel works as if in silence and solitude despite his own chanting. After a few more movements and long moments, the mohel stands upright, and looks to the father. "And where is the mother, please?" he said.

A path is cleared and the young woman moves to her husband's side. The mohel holds up the prayer book toward them and points to the appropriate place in the text. In quiet but steady voices, they speak, "Blessed are you, Lord our God, Ruler of the Universe, who made us holy through his commandments, and has commanded us to bring our son into the covenant of Abraham, our father." The room inhales in unison. Then the mohel lifts the filled cup in his right hand and recites the familiar blessing over the wine. He offers the cup to the mother and the father. The mohel dips his pinky finger into the wine and placed a drop on the child's lips. Then, on the mohel's prompt, everyone in the room recites: "Blessed are You, Lord our God, Ruler of the Universe, who has given us life, sustained us, and brought us to this time." This is the traditional blessing said on every festive occasion and holiday. It recognizes the contingency of this world and declares our knowledge that it is a mercy that we are alive and well enough to celebrate whatever the occasion might be for which we now are gathered. I have always respected this prayer for its humility and its joy. It is good to be alive.

The mohel lifts the child and hands the now quiet infant to his mother who hugs the child to her breast and kisses his head. It is time to name the child. The mohel says, "Our God and God of our fathers and mothers, preserve this child to his father and mother, and let his name be called in Israel Avel ben Aharon v'Hannah, Abel, son of Aaron and Hannah. May the father rejoice in the issue of his body, and the mother be glad with the fruit of her womb, as it is written, 'May your father and mother rejoice, and she who bore you be glad.'"

Then the mohel says, "May the parents rear their son to adulthood imbued with love of Torah and the performance of good deeds, and may they be privileged to bring him to the wedding canopy."

We respond, "Amen." Indeed, this was our wish: that the child study Torah and learn the commandments governing the covenant into which the child had been brought, that the child marry, or in more contemporary terms, find a partner to share his life, and learn to do good deeds. As this *brit milah* derived from God's covenant with Abraham, so would Abraham serve as the child's model. "For I have singled [Abraham] out so that he may instruct his children and his posterity to keep the way of the Lord by doing what is just and right." Then, looking at the child in his mother's arms, the mohel said, "With what can we bless you but with the riches of life; Eyes open wide to every flower and bird, Ears attentive to both the great and the meek. A smile of sunshine, feet to dance and hands to grasp. A heart that dreams and a soul that sings!"

The assembled respond, "Amen."

The Mohel looks to the parents, "Mazel tov." He smiles broadly. /*cresendo poco a poco*/ The singing starts behind me unobtrusively, peacefully, even somewhat plaintively. I recognize the song; my children had learned it in summer camp and long ago taught it to me. Sung in a minor key, as is so much Hebrew liturgy and song, the melody nonetheless contains expectation and possibility. At first, I recognize a single, female voice, Marsha's, the *shul* songstress. Others in the congregation know more liturgy and have studied more texts, but none has a voice as appealing as Marsha's. There is about it a sweetness and yet a depth. Not a classically trained voice but a pleasant one, she always sings in a key most could join—even I— and with little strain. Marsha is also a music teacher at a city elementary school. She sings: "*Kol ha-olam kulo gesher tsar m'od:*" The words mean: "All the world is a very narrow bridge," and derives from the liturgy of Rabbi Nachman of Bratslav, a dynamic, magnetic teacher who advocated that each person should speak to God as if to a friend in the language of daily life. *|cresendo poco a poco|* The line repeats: Marsha sings quietly yet invitingly, repeating the first line: "*Kol ha-olam kulo gesher tsar m'od.*" As she sings, next to her and immediately behind me, another woman adds her voice: "*Gesher tzar m'od. Gesher tzar m'od,*" *a very narrow bridge!* Ah, indeed it is, I think. And then from the other side of the assembled gathering, a third voice joins the song as the first line once again repeated, "*Kol ha-olam kulo gesher tsar m'od:*" and by the time the line has completed, several others begin to sing. I look around, and all attention seems intently focused on the child and his parents. A few close their eyes as they join in song. And some begin to sway.

The song then dramatically shifts tempo and register. Whereas the first lines are sung with little modulation, the second part of the song starts rhythmically and rises almost in supplication. *V'ha-ikar V'ha-ikar: most important, most important,* and now everyone, who has the least knowledge of it, has joined in song, and with all of the varied vocal keys and irregular tones and pitches the sound rises *|cresendo poco a poco|* transcendent and fills the yellow room. *Lo l'fachayd, lo l'fachayd klal,:* is not to be afraid at all! *All the world is a very narrow bridge. The most important part is not to be afraid at all.* More voices join in, and the mohel smiling, claps his hands in time. Several singers push to the front holding hands. With their free arms outstretched invitingly to either side, they dance around the child and his parents. The song's tempo and volume have increased considerably but not without melody, and those in the dance sing and smile broadly. *Kol ha-olam kulo gesher tzar m'od,* they sing. More step forward and join the celebration as the volume and the pace increase. Despite the words, the song is joyous and the dancing celebratory. *V-ha-ikar, V-ha-ikar, Lo l' fachayd, lo l' fachayd klal."* In the center of the circle of dancers, the child lies cradled in the arms of his parents who cradle each other. The dancing circle holds their delight. The most important part is not to be afraid at all.

I step forward and reach out my hand and voice to join the dance, and for the first time today, I feel myself honestly smile. I am not any better at dance than I am at song, but I can move my feet and my body in time. My voice approximates an appropriate key. I look about at the circle and my hands are clasped on either side by my friends. The broadness of the smiles enlarges the room and the tears that fill my eyes make the light sparkle. All are singing, and the room

is filled to its very corners in celebration. All the world is a very narrow bridge. The most important part is not to be afraid at all. There is nothing in the room except joy.
/*nobilmente*/ Amen.

FROM TIME AND PLACE...

ENDNOTES

11 New Criticism has its historical roots in England during the 1930s and was championed in the United States by John Crowe Ransom, Cleanth Brooks, Allen Tate, R.P. Blackmur and Robert Penn Warren. New Criticism assumes that in a close reading of the language of the artistic work a skilled reader would engage in an aesthetic experience that would lead to truth available only in that aesthetic experience. New Criticism arose in reaction to the development of the qualitative measures of science as the only source of truth.

12 "While men believed in the infinite . . . ": Henry David Thoreau, *The Annotated Walden*. Ed. Philip Van Doren (Barnes and Noble Books, 1992), p. 409.

13 "the first movement had two themes . . . ": http://www.hberlioz.com/Predecessors/beethsym.htm#sym8

13 "Only at rare intervals . . . " : http://www.hberlioz.com/Predecessors/beethsym.htm#sym8

13 "*The Grove Musical Dictionary* says, . . . ": *Grove Musical Dictionary of Music and Musicians, 2nd edition* (Macmillan Publishers Limited, 2001), p. 833.

14 "Thus, reader, I am myself . . . ": Michel de Montaigne, *The Complete Works*, Tr. Donald Frame (New York: Alfred Knopf, 1958), p. 2.

14 "A unique characteristic of the *Eroica* Symphony": Maynard Solomon, *Beethoven* (New York: Shirmer Books, 1979), p. 194.

15 "Beethoven's music does not merely express...": Solomon, p. 194.

16 "the ability to provide pleasure...": Sigmund Freud, *Jokes and Their Relation to the Unconscious* tr. James Strachey (New York: W.W. Norton & Company, 1960), p. 159.

17 "Ah, how beautiful...": Harvey Sachs. *The Ninth: Beethoven and the World in 1824* (New York: Random House, 2010), p. 118.

17 "Jacques Barzun has said...": Sachs, p. 118.

23 "A Klee painting...": Walter Benjamin, *Illuminations*. Tr. Walter Zohn (New York: Schocken Press), p. 257-8.

25 "Philip Roth writes...": Philip Roth, *Everyman* (New York: Houghton Mifflin Harcourt, 2006).

29 "*Yahrzeit*...": marks the anniversary of a death of a parent, spouse, child or sibling or some other family member, usually by lighting a memorial candle and reciting the Kaddish prayer.

31 I recall once reading that during meals Frederick Karl, *Kafka: Representative Man: Prague, Germans, Jews and the Crisis of Modernism* (New York: Fromm International, 1993).

32 "inhuman nature says to mankind": Henry David Thoreau, *The Maine Woods* (New York: Penguin Books, 1988), p. 86.

32 *niggun*: a wordless tune accompanying activity

34 "Go forth from your native land...": *Genesis* 12: 1-3

35 Perhaps Abram responds to "the unthought known," a concept derived from Christopher Bollas. The unthought known is knowledge that is not yet articulated, that which is known but has not yet been thought. Christopher Bollas, *The Shadow of the Object* (New York: Columbia University Press, 1987), p. 280. Raymond Williams refers to such knowledge as *structure of feeling*.

35 "Abram took his wife Sarai . . .": *Genesis* 12:5.

36 "Whenever we stumble in literary works . . .": Terry Eagleton, *The Trouble with Strangers* (Malden, MA, Wiley-Blackwell, 2009), p. 190.

37 "He ran from the entrance to the tent . . .": *Genesis* 18:2-5.

38 "And Isaac brought her": *Genesis*: 24:67.

39 "I will be with you and bless you . . .": *Genesis* 26:2-3.

40 "from the vicinity of Beer-lahai-roi . . .": *Genesis* 24:62.

40 "I have served your father . . .": *Genesis* 31:6.

40 "God was in this place . . .": *Genesis* 28:16.

40 "If God remains with me . . .": *Genisis* 28:20.

42 "Have you but one blessing, Father . . .": *Genesis* 27:36.

42 ". . . though there are alternative stories . . .": see Anita Diamont's novel *The Red Tent* (New York: Picador, 2007).

44 "All his sons and daughters . . .": *Genesis* 37:35.

45 The Story of the Prodigal Son: *Luke* 15:11-32.

45 "The son's leaving is . . .": Henry Nouwen, *The Return of the Prodigal Son: A Story of Homecoming* (New York: Image Books, 1994), p. 36.

49 "I am Esau . . .": *Genesis*, 27:19.

49 "I am your first born son . . .": *Genesis*: 27:32.

51 "Esau ran to greet him . . .": *Genesis* 33:4.

54 "I have stayed with Laban . . .": *Genesis* 32:4.

56 The reunion of Esau and Jacob: *Genesis* 33:1-17.

57 "Jacob journey to Succoth . . .": *Genesis* 32:17.

58 "If you are ready to leave . . .": Henry David Thoreau, *The Natural History Essays* (Salt Lake City: Peregrine Smith, 1980), p. 94.

58 "Home is where when you go there . . .": Robert Frost, "Death of the Hired Hand," in *Chief Modern Poets of England and America*, edited Gerald Dewitt Sanders, John Herbert Nelson, and M.L. Rosenthal (New York: The Macmillan Company, 1962), 78-II.

59 "All that we know of the self . . .": Abraham Joshua Heschel, *Between God and Man: An Interpretation of Judaism*, ed. Fritz A. Rothschild (New York: The Free Press, 1959), p. 62.

60 "It is not from experience . . .": Heschel. p. 65.

60 "The essence of what I am . . .": Heschel p. 62.

61 "To beguile the time . . .": William Shakespeare, *The Tragedy of Macbeth*, edited Irving Ribner and George Kittredge (Waltham and Company, Xerox College Publishing, 1971). I, v, 63.

62 "The fault dear Brutus . . .": William Shakespeare, *The Tragedy of Julius Caesar*, eds. Ribner and Kittredge, I, ii, 140-1.

65 "Because I could not stop for Death . . .": Emily Dickinson, in Sanders, Nelson and Rosenthal, p. II-21.

65 "This only applies where he does not turn . . .": *Babylonian Talmud*, Berakhot 6b.

70 "So it goes.": Kurt Vonnegut, *Slaughterhouse Five* (New York: Delacorte Press, 1969).

71 Maimonides held that a belief in the afterlife and the world to come was a principle article of the Jewish faith.

71 "For I will go down mourning . . .": *Genesis* 37:35.

71 The command to care for the widow, the orphan and the stranger in our midst is repeated almost three dozen times in Torah; this is a primary responsibility.

71 Ah, yes, I've come round to that opinion myself: a paraphrase from *Waiting for Godot*, Samuel Beckett (New York: Grove Press, 1961).

71 "this coyness lady were no crime . . . ": is from Andrew Marvell's poem, "To His Coy Mistress."

74 "Nothing to be done": *Waiting for Godot*, p. 1.

77 The custom of burying in shrouds is found in the *Babylonian Talmud*, Ketubot, 8b; of delivering food for the mourners in *Moed Katan*, 27a-b; and for drinks to be served in colored glass only in *Moed Katan*, 27a.

77 "Our masters taught . . . ": *Babylonian Talmud*, Pesachim, 54b.

79 "Yossarian's panicked cry . . . ": Joseph Heller, *Catch-22* (New York, Dell Publishing, 1961).

81 "The dead do not feel . . . ": *Babylonian Talmud*, Berakhot, 18b.

81 "When the soul leaves the body . . . ": in *The Book of Legends*, edited Hayim Nahman Bialik and Yehoshua Ravnitsky, tr. William C. Braude (New York: Schocken Books, 1992), p. 581

82 Koheleth cautions, "For the time of mischance . . . ": *Koheleth* 9:11.

82 Death of Aaron, *Numbers* 20:24-28.

83 "Should wicked Esau walk before her bier . . . ": in *The Book of Legends*, p. 50.

83 I found this narrative of the death of Aaron in *The Book of Legends*, p. 94-5.

84 God's final commands to Moses appear in *Deuteronomy* 31:14-26.

85 Death of Moses, *The Book of Legends*, p. 101-3.

88 "Fade far away . . . ": John Keats, "Ode to a Nightingale."

88 "a tale told by an idiot...": *Macbeth*. V, v, 26.

90 "How, if, when I am laid into the tomb...": *Romeo and Juliet*, William Shakespeare, IV, iii, 31-36.

90 "Does Kuhn not understand...": Primo Levi, *Survival in Auschwitz* (New York: Collier Books, 1961), p. 118.

92 "Only after 12 months...": *Babylonian Talmud.*, 58b.

93 "Treat every man according to his own deserts...": *Hamlet*, William Shakespeare, II, ii, 516.

101 "... the ability to provide pleasure...": Sigmund Freud, *Jokes and Their Relation to the Unconscious* tr. James Strachey (New York: W.W. Norton & Company, 1960), p. 159.

104 The story of Balaam: *Numbers* p. 22-24.

106 "He's supposed to be our merciful father...": Sholom Aleichem, *Tevye the Dairyman and the Railroad Stories*, tr. Hillel Halkin (New York: Schocken Books, 1996), p. 45.

107 "he would never have believed in False Profits...": Sholom Aleichem, p. 33.

120 Anna Wulf is the main character in Doris Lessing's novel *The Golden Notebook* (New York: Harper Perennial Classics, 2008).

120 "Ozymandias," a poem by Percy Bysshe Shelley.

121 "Do not entertain doubts...": Henry David Thoreau, *The Journal of Henry David Thoreau*, ed. Bradford Torrey and Francis J. Allen (New York: Dover Publications, 1962) Vol. II, p. 45.

121 "I do not know..." Thoreau, *Journal Vol. III* p. 208.

121 "In proportion as our inward life...": Henry David Thoreau, "Life Without Principle," *Thoreau, Collected Essays and Poems* (New York: Library Classics of the United States, 2001), p. 359.

122 "I considered my newspaper...": Benjamin Franklin, *The Autobiography of Benjamin Franklin* (New York: Signet, 1961), p. 108.

122 "In the conduct of my newspaper...": Franklin, p. 108.

122 "I could not fill their papers...": Franklin, p. 109.

123 ""some spirited remarks...": Franklin, p. 75.

124 "I repeat the testimony of many an intelligent foreigner...": Henry David Thoreau, "Slavery in Massachusetts," *Thoreau, Collected Essays and Poems* (New York: Library Classics of the United States, 2001), p. 340.

124 "If by liberty of the press were understood...": Thoreau, *Journal Vol. II*, p. 179.

124 "The last two Tribunes...": Thoreau, *Journal Vol. V*, p. 87.

124 "I am sure that I never read...": Henry David Thoreau, *The Annotated Walden* (New York, Barnes and Noble Books, 1970), p. 225.

127 "I know that there have been a few heroes in the land...": Thoreau, *Journal Vol. XII*, p. 413.

127 "Prominent and influential editors...": Thoreau, Journal *Vol XII*, p. 413.

128 "I wish to correct the tone and some of the statements..." Thoreau, *Journal Vol. XII*, p. 424.

128"I have read all the newspapers..." Thoreau, *Journal Vol. XII*, p. 435.

128 "Franklin,—Washington,—they were let off without dying...": Thoreau, *Journal Vol. XII*, p. 438.

128 *Human Events* http://www.humanevents.com/article.php?id= 23477, November, p. 19, 2007.

134 "Kennedy sent...": William Doyle, *An American Insurrection:*

James Meredith and the Battle of Oxford, Mississippi: 1962 (Anchor: New York), p. 247.

135 "a convoy of 161 vehicles . . . ": Doyle, p. 248-249.

143 "Think of your breed . . . ": qtd. in Primo Levi, *Survival in Auschwitz*, tr. Stuart Woolf (New York: Collier Books, 1961), p. 103.

144 "So it is with this calamity . . . ": Ralph Waldo Emerson, "Experience," *Nature and Selected Essays* (New York: Penguin Books, 2003), p. 288.

145 "Intellectual tasting of life . . . ": Emerson, p. 294.

145 "The native hue of resolution . . . ": *Hamlet*, William Shakespeare, edited Irving Ribner and George Kittredge (Waltham and Company, Xerox College Publishing, 1971). III, iii, 84-88.

152 "This is my covenant which you . . . ": *Genesis* 17:9.

156 Discussion is in *Babylonian Talmud*, Bava Bathra, 13a-14b.

158 I am indebted to Dr. Sheldon Berkowitz for his invaluable aid in my depiction of the ceremony of the *brit milah*. He is a superb mohel as well as a dedicated doctor.

163 Jack Wertheimer, "Pioneers of the Conservative Rabbinate: Reports from the Field by Graduates of 'Schechter's Seminary". Conservative Judaism, Conservative Judaism, Spring 1995. Rabbinical Assembly of America (RA). 1995: http://www.bjpa.org/Publications/details.cfm?PublicationID=943 . . .